A Rustle of Angels

The angels keep their ancient places,
Turn but a stone and start a wing!
'Tis ye, 'tis your estrangéd faces,
That miss the many-splendored thing.
—*Francis Thompson*

Stories About Angels
In Real-Life And Scripture

A Rustle of Angels

Marilynn Carlson Webber
&
William D. Webber

ZondervanPublishingHouse
Grand Rapids, Michigan

A Division of HarperCollins*Publishers*

Requests for information should be addressed to:
Zondervan Publishing House
Grand Rapids, Michigan 49530

Library of Congress Cataloging-in-Publication Data

Webber, William D.
    A rustle of angels : stories about angels in real life and
Scripture / by William D. Webber and Marilynn Carlson Webber.
        p. cm.
    Includes bibliographical references.
    ISBN 0-310-40500-9 (alk. paper)
    1. Angels. 2. Guardian angels. I. Webber, Marilynn Carlson.
    II. Title.
    BT966.2.W39   1993
    291.2'15—dc20   93–33916
                                                                    CIP

International Paper Edition: ISBN 0-310-40500-9

Edited by Mary McCormick
Cover design by Jim Connelly
Interior illustrations by Florence Chambers

94 95 96 97 98 / DH / 5 4 3

To our precious grandchildren
Aubrey Linnea and Angela Marie Webber,
who also believe in angels

To Marilynn's dear mother, Alice Carlson,
who taught her daughter to love God's angels
beginning in early childhood

To the wonderful people who have shared their
angel stories
that others might be blessed through this book.

Contents

Preface

One of the strangest discussions held in scholarly circles occurred in 1943. The *Encyclopaedia Britannica* decided to publish *The Great Books of the Western World* in a set that would make it easy for the serious individual to read the major books that had shaped our culture. The series was to become the basis for thousands of discussion groups.

The editorial board selected Mortimer J. Adler, one of the foremost philosophers of our time, to edit the work. To make the project more user-friendly, it was decided to select the great ideas that ran through the great books. Mortimer Adler would then write an essay about each idea, tracing its development through the centuries and explaining its importance. One hundred two great ideas were identified. Adler had little difficulty getting his associates to agree with almost all the ideas he proposed to include. The one exception was the subject of angels.

The publisher of the *Encyclopaedia Britannica* was Senator William Benton. He was flabbergasted that angels should be regarded as one of the great ideas. Robert Hutchins, president of the University of Chicago, and other members of the advisory board were also dubious about including angels, but Mortimer Adler was adamant. He pointed out that the subject of angels ran through the great books because their authors obviously considered angels of major importance. Adler found it curious that such a major idea was being currently ignored.

Ultimately, Mortimer Adler prevailed. The volume of essays on the great ideas was titled *The Syntopican*. The first article, "Angels," was 5000 words long.

In 1975 Billy Graham decided to preach a sermon on angels. To his surprise, he found very little in his library on the subject. As he continued his research, he was surprised to discover that very few books had been written about angels during this century. The book stores did have many books on demons, the occult, and the Devil. To fill the need, Billy Graham wrote the book *Angels, God's Secret Agents*. For months it topped the bestseller lists and went through several printings. In 1986 he brought out a revised and expanded edition.

Since that time there has been an explosion of interest in angels. Angel jewelry and figurines, once thought to be only for Christmas, can now be found in gift shops all year round.

The interest in angels has been reflected in popular television programs like *Highway to Heaven*. Talk shows have featured programs on angels. The Associated Press wrote an article carried in newspapers across the country on the growing interest in angels, quoting Marilynn as having said, "Open the pages of Scripture, and there's a rustle of angels." With the new interest in angels many books are now on the market. Why, then, another book on angels?

Because the increasing interest in angels has also resulted in confusion about the nature and ministry of angels, many of the books and articles written on the subject contain conflicting ideas. There is a need for a book that not only relates angel experiences but also clearly presents the teachings of the Bible. This book, then, is more than a story book—it is a book of popular biblical theology, beginning with the experiences that people have reported to us, then comparing these experiences with the Scriptures.

A Rustle of Angels is filled with true stories, unlike the fictive stories often found in the tabloids. In most cases the stories are based on the written accounts of real persons with definite addresses, and actual names are used except in a few cases where the use of names could be a problem to others. Where real names are not used, the book so indicates.

The paramount purpose of this book is to glorify God by telling of his love and care as seen in the ministry of his angels and to encourage people by letting them know that angels are still ministering today.

Our thanks to our daughter, Sharon Linnea Scott, for her professional advice and substantial contributions to the text; to our son, Stephen Webber, for his encouragement; and to Robert Scott for his assistance in the early stages of the book.

We have been strengthened and encouraged by those who have prayed for us and this book. Those prayer warriors and those leading prayer groups include Evelyn Christenson, Joan Wester Anderson, Ruth Smith Patrice Verhiner, Lucille Calvert, Virginia Cosner, Jane Eastman, Betty Ford, Carolynn Crowe, Margaret Sharp and the Mission Angels Group, Mary Matthews, Cofounder of the Angel Collectors Club of America, and the congregation of the Grand View Baptist Church, Grand Terrace, California.

If you have felt the rustle of an angel's wing in your life, we shall be pleased to hear from you. As we share our experiences, we give glory to God, and others are blessed.

William and Marilynn Carlson Webber
275 Celeste Drive
Riverside, CA 92507

Chapter
1

An Explosion of Interest in Angels

Even the *Wall Street Journal* noticed it: There has been an explosion of interest in angels. Angels are not a new fad—they've been around for a long time. Open the pages of Scripture, and there's a rustle of angels. They appear in the Bible over three hundred times, popping up in the most unlikely places and doing unexpected things. Here are a few of their biblical roles: ladder climbers, wrestlers, lion tamers, weight lifters, birth announcers, recruiters, warriors, executioners, rescuers, and comforters.

Why are people talking about them now more than ever before? There are many theories. People were once afraid to talk about an angel experience for fear that others would consider them to be a bit strange. Today people do speak more openly of personal experiences, especially spiritual experiences, sharing their angel experiences on television talk shows, in magazine articles and books, and reading about angels in their daily newspapers. Today it's safer to come out of the angelic closet.

Some think that angels are more active today. It may be that God is working out his purposes, and in his divine plan this is a period when angels are given more to do. They may be preparing us for the next chapter that God will write in history.

We may be hearing more about angels today because of all the personal and world problems we are facing. When life is easy, people tend to become complacent and self-sufficient. The more self-reliant we are, the less open we are to God and the supernatural, but when life comes tumbling in and we cry out for help beyond ourselves, God does respond, sometimes using the ministry of angels. Besides, when we are open to God, we are more likely to recognize the work of angels in situations that previously we might have attributed to coincidence.

Perhaps the best explanation is that ours is a scientific age. In school many of us were taught that when we learned enough facts, we would be able to solve our problems and live happily ever after. People have found that science does not have the answers for many of life's problems. While science is helpful in many ways, it just isn't enough. Humans are designed with a spiritual hunger, a sense of wonder; therefore, people have become increasingly open to the spiritual and are willing to accept the reality of angels.

For decades, Marilynn has been fascinated with angels. She enjoys an extensive angel collection (ranging from the weather vane atop our house to the angel-shaped toilet flusher in the bath, with two thousand or so in between). Over the years she has spoken about angels to diverse groups, from the national convention of the Angel Collectors Clubs of America and The Angels of the World International to local women's clubs and church groups. She is widely known as "the angel lady."

As a minister and student of the Scriptures, Bill also knows there are many things that angels are not. For example, they are not what humans become after death—angels are created as angels. Nor are they cute, cuddly beings—ours to command. In fact, in the Scriptures nearly every angelic appearance begins with the angel's having to say the same thing: "Fear not!" All who have had a true angel encounter find that they have been changed—that there is a new level of wonder and awe in their lives. Something more has been revealed to them: something more about creation, yes—but more important, something about the nature of God.

Where did our interest in angels begin? For Marilynn the love of angels began when she was four years old. Bedtime was a difficult experience because she was afraid of the dark. Her mother tried everything to calm Marilynn's childish fears but without success. Then one night before her mother tucked her into bed she said, "Marilynn, I have a surprise for you." First, Mother Carlson read from the ninety-first Psalm: "For he shall give his angels charge over thee, to keep thee in all thy ways" (v. 11). Next she explained that God had appointed an angel to be Marilynn's guardian angel and that even when Marilynn slept, the angel kept careful watch over her. Then her mother reached into a bag and took out an angel figurine. Made of plaster, it was about five inches tall. When she placed it on the dresser, Marilynn thought it the most beautiful thing she had ever seen.

I will always keep it, Marilynn thought to herself. Comforted by the thought of a guardian angel, she fell fast asleep during which her fear of the dark was overcome. Although she now has many fine collectible angels, her first angel is her most prized possession.

As Marilynn grew older, she never lost her belief in guardian angels. When she was fourteen, her parents moved from Chicago to suburban Wheaton, Illinois. Inasmuch as it was near the end of the school term, Marilynn stayed with a friend and attended classes at Austin High School. On weekends she took the train to her new home in Wheaton. One Friday just before she boarded the Chicago and Northwestern train for the trip home, Marilynn learned that her friend and Sunday school teacher had cancer and only a short time to live. Marilynn was in shock as she rode the train. Death had never been a reality for her. It was something for old people, and so far, for old people whom she did not really know. The thought that this young adult, her friend, was going to die was difficult for this high school freshman to accept. Marilynn tried to comfort herself with the thought of heaven, but as the train made its thirty-mile journey, her sadness grew more profound.

By habit she got off the westbound train at the College Street Station. Lost in thought, she slowly began to cross the eastbound tracks on her way home. Suddenly she heard the loud rumbling of a steam locomotive and heard the frightening blast of a train whistle. She was on the tracks, and the oncoming train was so close that she could see the blue eyes and the terrified face of the engineer. Paralyzed with fear, Marilynn was unable to move. *I'm going to die*, she thought. *I'll be in heaven before my Sunday school teacher is.*

Just an instant before the train would have hit her, Marilynn was pushed. Even now she remembers it well. "It was as if a giant shoved me from behind, and I went flying off the tracks and fell on the cinders just below." She scrambled to her feet, grateful to be alive, and wondering who the hero was that had saved her life.

No one was there! There was not a person in sight. At that moment Marilynn knew that her life had been saved by her guardian angel. There was no other explanation. She hurried home. When she met her mother, her words tumbled out as she recounted her close brush with death and her rescue by her guardian angel, but it was a long time before Marilynn was able to tell others about her encounter. "Partly because it was so personal, so sacred," she says, "but also because I was concerned that people wouldn't believe me—they'd think that I'm strange." Although she kept these things to herself and pondered them in her heart, it was a life-changing experience.

Even as a young theology student, Bill had an interest in angels. His interest, too, began in a personal way. During his junior year at Wheaton College he was away on a debate trip during class registration. He chose his classes and asked the girl he was dating, Marilynn Carlson, to register for him. His choice for physical education was wrestling. Marilynn was appalled. She knew nothing about college wrestling. The glimpses she had seen of professional wrestling on TV had convinced her that it is a dangerous sport, so she enrolled him in tumbling instead.

When Bill returned from the debate trip, it was too late to change classes, so with sincere prayers for survival he attended classes. Though a fair wrestler, Bill's six-foot-two inch body was never made for tumbling. The only thing that saved him were the precautions taken in class. When a student worked out on the trampoline, for example, there was always another person present called a "spotter" whose responsibility was to spot possible problems and keep the tumbler from injury. If the tumbler was coming down headfirst, the spotter would tap him on the shoulder so that he would be able to turn and land on his feet—a precaution that the top tumblers never needed. For Bill, the spotter's intervention was almost routine.

To help finance his education, Bill was working at night, cleaning the exterior of railroad cars in the Chicago, Aurora, and Elgin railway train yard in Wheaton. One night as he worked alone on a high, wet scaffold, his foot slipped. He plunged headfirst to the concrete pavement below. Even as he fell, he knew that he was probably going to die, but just before he hit the ground he felt a strong tap on his shoulder. Instinctively using his training from the tumbling class, he righted himself. He landed on his feet. Turning to thank the spotter, he found himself alone in the train yard. No one was there. Yet the tap on his shoulder had been unmistakable. It had come just at the right time, in the right place, with just the right force. An unseen spotter had saved his life. Bill knew that it was an angel.

A mighty push. A tap on the shoulder. In the coming pages you'll find these to be far from the most dramatic angel experiences. Yet for each of us they weren't only life-saving—they were life-changing.

This is a book of practical wonder in which we will explore the nature of angels through present-day encounters and biblical stories. All of the stories in this book have come directly from the original sources. The ones we've accepted have all been checked against biblical criteria of what angels are and do. In each, we urge you to read and decide for yourself. This book will also give you the means to become an angel sleuth yourself, to be able to recognize real angel activity, and discern what is not.

We introduce you to people in these pages to give you strength and inspiration and to excite you about the nature of God, who has more to show us than we can "ask or even imagine."

True Confessions

Of all people, it was philosopher Mortimer J. Adler who wrote that angels are more fascinating than science fiction and extraterrestrial beings. Truth *is* stranger than fiction. Consider the following.

Angels were very active in the Bible, some of whose most exciting stories are about angels. The Saturday cartoon shows on TV cannot top Daniel in the lion's den with the surprise ending of an angel's appearing to close the mouths of the ferocious beasts. Or the story of Peter in prison on death row, guarded by sixteen soldiers and double-chained between two guards—then suddenly, dramatically rescued by an angel.

Many people have no difficulty believing that in biblical times God used angels to do his work. There is an easy acceptance of the angels who announced the birth of Jesus to the shepherds at the first Christmas. The same people may be surprised or even skeptical when they hear that people today, especially friends they know, tell of encounters with angels.

Such hesitation is understandable. The biblical accounts happened long ago. We think of the people in the Bible as saints who belong in stained-glass windows, not as ordinary people like our relatives or neighbors. Besides, the happenings in the Bible were important, of eternal consequence (Isn't that why they are in the Good Book?). But would God send his angels today to the insignificant people living in unnoticed neighborhoods, who live out their lives in the commonest conditions of routine work, typical daily activities, and obscurity? Surely in the past God may have chosen to use his angels to perform his mighty acts. We might even concede that on rare occasions his angels might be pressed into duty today if there were some event of extreme importance that could only be handled by a supernatural intervention. But is it believable that an angel might intervene in my life or the life of my neighbor? Especially if I were not sent to worship the Christ child in the manger, or to be asked to carry out a task of eternal significance?

Yes! God does use his angels today—sometimes for assignments that seem important. But the eyewitness evidence points to the fact that God's angels are frequently at work, often in the most ordinary events of life.

If this is true, why don't we hear of it more often? Many of those we have talked with tell us that this experience is an encounter with the holy. The fact that they have met an angel lifted that event to the sacred. For some this sacredness is a "secret" that ought not to be shared with scoffers.

It is similar to the finding of Carl Jung, the famous psychoanalyst, when he visited the Pueblo Indians: He noted that the most sacred events in the religious life of the Native Americans were kept absolutely secret to outsiders. It was not that they were embarrassed or ashamed. Rather, according to the Native American reasoning, to divulge the secrets of "the holy" would be to compromise the integrity of the worshiper and the tribe. No white person was invited to their worship, and no white person was told what went on in their ritual times.

In a similar way, those who have met an angel have found the experience to be so intensely personal, so private, that it was not to be shared indiscriminately.

Some told no one. Others told a parent or spouse. Some shared it with their church group. A few would tell anyone willing to listen.

If people keep these angel experiences to themselves, then how did such experiences find their way into this book? Here an analogy to Scripture may be helpful. Mary, the mother of Jesus, had an encounter with the angel Gabriel. The shepherds told her of the heavenly host who had told them of the birth of her child. Mary's response is found in Luke 2:19: "But Mary treasured up all these things and pondered them in her heart." Apparently at first these things were too sacred for Mary to talk about. Later it was helpful to share her experiences so that others would grow in their faith in Jesus Christ. Finally, Mary's experiences would become an important part of the gospel records.

In a similar way, for many whose personal experiences are recounted in this book, the events have been treasured and held close to the heart. There was a secret longing to disclose the occurrence, but at the right time, in the right way, to the right person. It was to be told so that others could have their faith strengthened and that glory be given to God.

We share this conviction. When the staff of the television series *Unsolved Mysteries* asked us to open our files and give them stories for their program, we turned them down. Angels are not "unsolved mysteries" to be placed in the same context as questionable paranormal activity.

How did we find these stories, then? For the most part, we did not find them—they found us.

Marilynn wrote a moving, true-life story about a woman whose life had been changed by an angel. The story was published in the October 1992 issue of *Guideposts* magazine. David Briggs of the Associated

Press, writing an article on the explosion of interest in angels, interviewed Marilynn. The account of her experience with an angel and her comments about angels were carried in large metropolitan newspapers and hundreds of hometown papers. Marilynn's experience with an angel, related in the introduction of this book, was printed in the December 1992 issue of the *Ladies' Home Journal*.

We were unprepared for the response because although we have read newspapers and magazines for years, we ourselves have never written to an author in response to what we read.

People began to call, usually long distance. A call from Maine would be followed by one from California. Frequently the caller would say, "I've never felt so compelled to call someone in my life, but after reading your story I know that you would understand." Then they would share a beautiful account of their own experience with an angel.

Thousands of letters began to arrive. Hundreds had first-person accounts of angels. Often they began with the words, "I've never told this to anyone before," but as we read the letters it was easy to see that their story had to be told. Their lives had been touched by an angel, and they were no longer the same. Because Marilynn, too, had experienced the brush of an angel's wings, they felt that she would understand and believe their experience. They also recognized Marilynn as an author with a wide audience, who wrote of experiences with angels in a factual but reverent manner. The implicit request was that what God had done for them might be shared in an appropriate way so that others, too, might rejoice with them and give glory to God. This is the trust we are trying to keep as we recount their stories.

Chapter 3

Do You Have a Guardian Angel?

From time to time Margy thought about angels. She knew they were in the Bible, but if they existed then, did they still exist now? And if angels do exist, do they still do things in our world?

Cattle ranching is hard work, but at times it is absolutely delightful. Margy and Jared Nesset on horseback were checking their cow herd. The Wyoming mountains were breathtaking; the summer day was glorious. As husband and wife they were enjoying the day, enjoying their horses, and enjoying each other's company. Suddenly something spooked Margy's horse. He reared and sunfished, throwing Margy from the saddle, with one foot still caught in the stirrup.

No matter how experienced a rider is, there is nothing he can do in such a situation to avoid serious injury. The expected outcome would be for Margy to make a crash landing on the rocks and be injured further because her horse would drag her until she could free her foot from the stirrup.

In this instance, Margy felt no pain. Instead she found herself cradled in soft, unseen arms and gently lowered to the ground. She felt more like a child being placed in a featherbed than a woman falling from a horse onto a bed of rocks. Immediately she scrambled to her feet, unaided, because she wasn't hurt. She rushed to Jared, excitedly telling him of the wonderful sensation she had had of being gently cradled through her fall. Jared is the logical thinker of their family, and Margy didn't know how much of her strange tale he would buy, but she was so excited that she couldn't keep silent. She knew that it had to have been her guardian angel who had caught her in mid-air, freed her from the stirrup, and tenderly laid her on the ground. She *knew* what she had experienced.

Jared knew what he had seen. He had watched helplessly as his wife's horse pitched her off—fearful as he saw her foot still caught in the stirrup. He expected the horse to drag her violently across the rough rocks, but as soon as she was dethroned from the saddle, Jared saw everything change into slow motion, "like the rerun of a football play," he said. He saw the violent movements of the horse, but in slow motion they appeared peaceful. As an accomplished horseman, Jared knew that horses do not buck slowly, thus he watched in amazement as he saw his wife almost float to the ground, with one deft movement freeing her foot from the stirrup.

Ask Margy today what she believes, and she will answer with confidence: "Angels *are*. They do exist. They continue to do their work with ease, agility, and a preciseness that defies even the law of gravity when necessary. My own guardian angel? Yes, you had better believe it. For myself, there was absolutely no room for doubt. I had no option but to believe it. I am so thankful for that experience—an experience that didn't break my back but only opened my eyes."

Today, because of her personal experience, Margy is convinced that she has a guardian angel. For each story that follows there are many more in our files of people who believe in angels because they themselves have encountered one. And our research is just the tip of the iceberg: There are thousands of people in the United States who are absolutely certain that they have been helped by an angel.

Jesus, in Matthew 18:10 said, "See that you do not

look down on one of these little ones. For I tell you that
their angels in heaven always see the face of my Father
in heaven." Implicit in the words of Christ is the fact
that every child has a guardian angel. Other biblical
references, such as Psalm 34:7, indicate that the angels
continue their watchcare over an individual for life. As
Basil the Great wrote in A.D. 379, every one of the
faithful has a guardian angel. The theologian Thomas
Aquinas said that at birth every person is given a
guardian angel who continually lights, guards, rules, and
guides.

Two Flew Over the Handlebars

Joyce Brown was riding her bicycle, coming home
from work in the late afternoon. The Arizona sun was
low on the horizon, making visibility difficult for
everyone on the street. Joyce peddled to the intersection,
where there was a stop sign. Instead of making a
complete stop, she eased around the corner and was hit
from behind by a truck whose driver did not see her.
Joyce flew over the handlebars. Although she was not a
Christian, she cried out, "Jesus! Help me!"

Immediately Joyce felt herself being cushioned, as
though she were wrapped in pillows. When she landed,
witnesses said she bounced like a person landing on a
trampoline. Joyce felt no pain. As a precaution she went
to the hospital, where a thorough check revealed no
serious injuries. Ask Joyce for an explanation, and she
will tell you that those pillows were angels gently
carrying her. In gratitude, Joyce began a spiritual quest
that brought her to faith in the same Jesus who had
answered her emergency prayer.

When the Surf Is Up

After graduating from high school, Phillip Howell was living in Hawaii. Surfing was more than an interest—it was a passion. The North Shore of Kauai is a surfer's paradise, and Phillip regularly rode the waves.

A strong swimmer, his ten years of experience had given him skill in using the board. Skill was needed in the thirty-foot waves that were common on the North Shore. The swell would come in, hit a reef from the deep water, and a vast amount of water would break with enormous power. That was the excitement that Phil loved. To catch the best waves meant that a surfer would venture as much as a mile from shore. To be sure that he didn't accidentally lose his board, it was attached by a strap or leash to his ankle. Phillip was on his board, paddling out, when a "clean-up set" came in. A clean-up set breaks farther out than anyone expects. Its size and force is so tremendous that it takes everybody in with it.

Seeing the clean-up wave coming, Phillip sat on his board, trying to get his ankle free of the leash that held it to the board so that he could dive to the bottom for protection, but the wave broke directly over him with the lip right on top of him. Usually the crest of a wave is only a foot or two thick. To his dismay, Phillip saw about twelve feet of water coming over him. He knew that even strong swimmers had drowned when caught in the force of a clean-up wave.

Unable to get free of the leash, Phillip dived off his board, waiting to be crushed by the sheer wall of water but instead found himself flying through the air—and through the back of the wave—with his board flying parallel with him! To his great amazement he felt himself being carried—propelled at great speed— through the back of the wave. From where he had been on his board to the wall of the wave was about thirty feet, yet Phillip found himself passing through the wall of water almost instantaneously, as though there were a tunnel through the thousands of gallons of water. He felt no pressure of the water as he passed through even though there is no natural way that a person can make his way through a thirty-foot wave.

Yet Phillip found himself out of danger in the back of the wave. He scrambled on his board and made his way to shore, confident that his guardian angel had opened the wave and carried him through it.

Since then Phillip has talked to every pro he could find, asking if this has ever happened to anybody else. They listen to his story and reply that they know of nothing even close to his experience. There is no explanation other than that a guardian angel saved Phillip's life, taking him through the wall of the wave without injury.

They Shall Bear Thee Up in Their Hands

Shirley Halliday opened her Bible. It was a regular part of her daily routine, and this day she especially felt that she needed a word from God. Her work as a nurse was rewarding but tiring, and at times like this she missed her husband the most. He had died only three months ago.

Tonight the house was quiet. Her thirteen-year-old daughter, Janie, was on vacation with her oldest brother, his wife, and their two children. Shirley read Psalm 91 in her worn King James Bible. She read verses eleven and twelve, "For he shall give his angels charge over thee, to keep thee in all thy ways. They shall bear thee up in their hands, lest thou dash thy foot against a stone."

Shirley stopped reading and burst into tears, sobbing almost uncontrollably. She felt that Janie was in danger but did not know how or where—only that her daughter was in a situation in which she might die.

Shirley began pleading with the Lord. "I know you never give us more than we can bear," she prayed, "but I know I couldn't bear losing my daughter so soon after my husband's death. I place Janie in your care."

Shirley prayed in the words of the *Episcopalian Prayer Book*: "I entrust all who are dear to me to Thy never-failing care and love, in this life and the life to come, for you know better things than I to do for them. O God, I truly place my daughter Janie in your hands." She prayed with all the passion of a mother who knows that her daughter's life is in the balance. Then she claimed Psalm 34:4: "I sought the Lord, and he heard me, and delivered me from all my fears."

Shirley felt the burden lifted from her, then a feeling of peace swept over her. She knew that the Lord had heard her pleas and answered her prayers.

Shirley continued to read Psalm 91. Two verses later she read, "He shall call upon me, and I will answer him." It came as a complete confirmation to her. The peace had come even before she had read the promise of God's answer. Now she praised God with her whole heart.

Miles away, Janie was trying to photograph the sights of the Grand Canyon and the Painted Desert. In the area of the Petrified Forest, anxious for a better picture, she left the family group, climbed over a barrier, and went to the edge of a cliff. The ground was covered with what looked like black ashes. Janie slipped and went over the edge. She plummeted down, frantically reaching for something—anything—to hold onto. There was nothing. The walls of the canyon were black like asphalt. As Janie looked down, it was all black and seemed bottomless. It seemed to the teenager that she would be seriously hurt.

Then she felt a *presence*. Janie stopped falling, suddenly coming to a complete stop as though she had been caught. Janie put her hand out and felt the slippery wall of the canyon. She tried to turn her body, but all that happened was that she felt herself dropping some more. Carefully trying to edge her way up, she would only slide farther down. It seemed impossible. There was no way she could climb back up, and she was in danger of falling the rest of the way to the bottom.

Janie felt enveloped with the *presence*. Suddenly she found herself back at the top. She knew that she had not climbed back up on her own. That would have been impossible. She could only explain that an angel had stopped her fall by catching her in his strong arms. She had been lifted to the top on the wings of angels.

Not wanting to frighten her mother, Janie did not mention her close call when she phoned home that night. "We're having a wonderful time, and we're all okay," she reported.

"I know you will all be safe," her mother replied. "I've placed you in the hands of the Lord."

At that time neither mother nor daughter told of the experience each had had a short time earlier.

When the family returned home, they were recounting the adventures on their trip. Passing one picture to her mother, Janie said, "Here's the place I fell."

"What do you mean?" her mother answered. "How did you fall? Tell me about it."

Janie recounted her close brush with death and the mysterious rescue.

"When did it happen?" the mother asked.

"The day we visited the Grand Canyon. You know I called home later that night."

"But exactly when did it happen that day?" Shirley persisted.

The vacationers remembered the time of the accident. *It was the exact time that Shirley had made her fervent pleas to God.*

Shirley will always remember that day. "It was no coincidence," she states with assurance. "It was the Holy Spirit who let me know that Janie's life was in danger. When I cried out to God in prayer, he sent his angels to rescue Janie. I read Psalm 91 again in the *Living Bible* and it fit exactly, "For he orders his angels to protect you wherever you go. They will steady you with their hands to keep you from stumbling against the rocks on the trail."

Janie is no longer a teenager. Shirley Halliday is now Shirley Rhodes, having married a wonderful husband. "God is so good," she declares.

Angel on the Cowcatcher

William "Bill" Henry was at the throttle of the Buffalo Flyer, PG-16. The steam locomotive had stopped at Port, Pennsylvania, and filled its tanks with water. The night express was running at full speed just above Shickshinny where the mining region begins, when the engineer was startled to see a man on the cowcatcher. Bill watched in amazement as the man swung confidently up onto the steam chest. Holding on to the handrail with his left hand, he used his right hand to give the railroad signal, *CAUTION—STOP!*

Bill called to Henry Sulenk, the fireman: "Hank, it looks like we have a passenger!"

Hank looked out and said, "Probably a bum that got on at Port."

The man stepped onto the running board that led from the front of the engine to the cab, all the while giving a signal, now *DANGER—STOP!*

The engineer watched with fascination. The train was running with a full head of steam. The forward movement of the engine created a strong wind, yet this man was walking toward the cab with no difficulty.

It was strange, too, about his clothes. He was dressed in a light gray suit and wore a soft Fedora hat, but the wind did not blow his clothes, and his Fedora did not move from his head. As he came closer, Bill Henry could see him clearly. The man had a light-brown mustache, but it was his eyes that Bill would never forget—they seemed filled with compassion and wonder.

Now the strange rider changed the sign to read: *EMERGENCY—STOP!*

The engineer released the throttle, put on all the brakes, and the Buffalo Flyer ground to a hard stop. Bill Henry whistled for the flagmen. Immediately they went into their emergency procedure of placing flags on the tracks to warn other trains that there was a halted locomotive. One flagman went to the back to place his warning flags. The engineer watched the other flagman hurrying to place his flags in front of the train. Peering into the darkness, Bill saw the flagman stop about 150 feet ahead and signal with his lantern: *CAVE-IN!*

When the crew rushed ahead, they found a gaping hole where the tracks had been.

Realizing how close they had come to death, the crew hurried back to thank the mysterious night rider. He had disappeared as mysteriously as he had appeared and was never found.

Bill Henry seldom talked about the mysterious rider on the Buffalo Flyer, but when he did, he always let his listener decide who the man in gray might be. But Bill himself had no doubts. He was certain that the "man" was an angel from God.

Chapter
4

Guardians Angels: To Light, To Guard, To Rule, To Guide

Carmen Mechikoff—the Mexican Taxi

Carmen grew up in a colony in Mexico with her parents, four sisters, and one brother. Her mother, Rosario, was a very intelligent, hard-working, and God-fearing woman. Carmen describes her mother's faith in God as amazing and remembers her as always reaching out to others in kindness and love. But her family was always Rosario's first priority.

As others saw him, Carmen's father was a friendly, outgoing man, well-liked in the community. When the family moved to the colony, he became friends—more accurately, "drinking buddies"—with the neighbors next door.

At home, Carmen's father was very demanding and often abusive, especially when he had been drinking. One day after drinking with the man next door, he came home after dark. There was a terrible row. Even now Carmen remembers hearing her mother scream and how she and the other children rushed in, trying to save their mother from serious injury. His anger spent, Carmen's father stormed out of the house into the darkness. He worked from 10:00 P.M. to 6:00 A.M. at a filling station some distance away.

It was clear that life could not go on like this. Carmen's mother decided that now was the time to bring an end to the vicious cycle of violence in the home.

The best way, she thought, was to reason with the neighbor next door, so she went to the neighbor and told the man that it was not right for him to encourage her husband to drink. "Look what happened," she said, showing him some of the bruises she had received.

Instead of listening and being reasonable, the man next door became very upset. Angrily he said, "I'm going to go and get your husband. He'll know how to deal with you."

It was no idle threat. Carmen had often heard her father say that he never wanted his family to embarrass him in front of others. What went on in their house was to be kept a secret from everyone else. If anyone told, her father said, he would do something drastic to them. Now Carmen's mother had broken the code of silence. The enraged neighbor was on his way to her husband's place of work. Her husband would come home, Carmen's mother knew, and the earlier abuse would be mild compared with what would follow. She feared for her life.

Rosario rushed into their home. "Start packing!" she ordered the children. Turning to her teenage daughter and eleven-year-old son, she said, "Go out and try to find a taxi."

The children knew that the streets would be deserted, that it was unsafe to be out in the colony after dark, and that because of this there were no taxis, especially in the area of town where they lived. They could also see the desperation of their mother, and they knew how violent their father could be. Desperate times call for drastic measures. The two children did not argue. Going out on the dangerous streets seemed less of a risk than meeting their enraged father when he came home.

To their surprise they found a car with two young men waiting in the street. The strangers came into the home and immediately took charge. No explanations were needed—the men knew what was needed without being told. They supervised the packing of clothing and helped carry things to the car. Everyone in the family listened to them and responded immediately. Feeling that they were being rescued, they gave their implicit trust to two people they had never before seen.

One of the men said, "Hurry! Hurry!"

Quickly the family rushed out to the car. "Hurry up!" the man insisted. "He's almost here."

They crammed into the car: mother, six children piled three-high on each other's laps, the two men and a cage with two birds wedged somewhere on top. The driver started the car and pulled quickly into the street. The family froze as they saw the vehicle with their father coming toward them. Instinctively they tried to hide, but there is no place to hide in a car filled with nine people. They saw their father, but he did not notice their car as it passed. Was it because he was not expecting his family to leave and thus paid no attention to a passing car? Or was it because he was so consumed with his anger? Or was it divine intervention?

They drove quite a distance in silence until they came to the house of one of Rosario's friends. In a few words the mother told her friend what had happened. "Come in, come in, you can stay here!" the friend invited.

The family tumbled out of the car, each one (except the baby) carrying in some of their belongings. The two men brought in what was left. Rosario turned to thank her benefactors, but they were not there. She hurried out the door. The car was not there, nor was it to be seen on the street. They had had no time to drive away, and Rosario could see the deserted street for some distance.

"It's strange," Carmen states as she recounts the story. "Our family was saved by two men, but we do not remember what their faces looked like. All we can remember is that there was a kindness and love that radiated from their faces. We instinctively knew that we could trust them with our lives. When we were safe and had time to think, we asked several questions. How was it they were there waiting with a car? How did they know what needed to be done without being told? Why did we follow their directions without question? How could they know that my father was almost home? How could two men and a car disappear?"

Their mother, a woman of deep faith, knew the answer. "They were angels," she said. Carmen has never doubted her.

Joyce Talmachoff—Angels in Goblin Valley

Joyce enjoyed exploring new places with her motor home. On this day she had set out with her mother and her daughter, both named Mary, to see Goblin Valley, Utah. It was a beautiful day without a cloud in the sky.

The road into Goblin Valley was in poor repair. It was like driving on a washboard, and Joyce was concerned because the motor home was continually being jarred. Her mother, reading the map, said, "There is another road on the map. If you'd like to try it, I'm game, but it's up to you."

"Let's go for it," Joyce said. When she turned off, the road was smooth, but it soon became sandy. From time to time they crossed the dry creek beds and Joyce could feel the back of the motor home fishtail a little bit but not enough to be concerned about. It appeared to be a good, sandy road.

As they turned a corner next to a rock embankment crossing another dry creek bed, the motor home got stuck in the sand. Joyce was unable to get the motor home to move forward or back. It wouldn't even rock. It was stuck, hopelessly stuck in the sand. They were alone in the middle of nowhere. It was quite possible that no one might travel that way for days. Joyce's mother decided that she would hike to see if she could find some help.

Joyce got out and surveyed the problem. At that time Joyce was not a strong Christian, but it occurred to her there was nothing she could do—except pray. So down on their knees they went, mother and daughter, kneeling in the sand, repeating the prayer they knew, the Lord's Prayer. As best as they knew how, they committed the situation to the Lord.

It was fewer than ten minutes later when a four-wheel-drive jeep rounded the curve in the road. The driver stopped, got out of his jeep, and asked, "What are you doing out here all by yourself?"

"I'm not alone," Joyce answered. "My daughter is with me, and I know that God is with me. I'm not alone."

"I've been sent here to help you," the stranger explained matter-of-factly.

Joyce told him that her mother was hiking down the road, looking for help. "First, we've got to go find your mother," the good Samaritan said. Off he went, and in a few minutes returned with Mary.

The man tied a rope to the back of the motor home, then fastened it to the jeep. "Put your engine in reverse" he instructed. The four-wheel-drive kicked in, the jeep pulled on the rope, and slowly the motor home was freed from the sand. It was not an easy feat, but with his help Joyce was able to turn the motor home around.

Joyce was overjoyed. She wanted to give the stranger something for helping them, but he refused. "At least let me fix you lunch," Joyce offered.

"Okay," the man replied.

Joyce prepared lunch. As they were eating, she had the feeling that she was really entertaining an angel.

After lunch the man said, "You got stuck once on this sandy road. Let me follow you to be sure you will make it back to the main road."

The three women looked at each other and nodded in unison. They had had enough adventures for one day. With the jeep a few feet behind, the motor home started back down the sandy road. Joyce kept watching it in her rearview mirror. As they came to the main road, she leaned out the window to wave good-bye, but the jeep and its driver had disappeared. There had been no side road where the jeep could have turned off. It had been there, close behind Joyce; then it was gone.

This event changed Joyce's life. "If God loves me enough to send me angels to help me," Joyce explains, "then I need to dedicate my life to the Lord. Ever since then I have truly tried to make God number one, and he has directed my life."

Samantha and the Angel in the Middle

Samantha from New York State told us the following story:

"When I was eight-and-a-half months pregnant, my husband and his mother got into a terrible fight. It was in our apartment, in a hallway that was very small—maybe eight feet by four feet. As the yelling escalated out of control, I stepped between them to try to calm them down.

"My husband was in a rage, and he reached around me and started to choke his mother. I knew that I had put myself—and my unborn child—in harm's way, and I said a desperate prayer for protection. I remember a flash of bright light; then a peace and a kind of numbness came over me. I distinctly felt something wrap around me and my baby. I knew that there were arms around me, of course—my husband's—but I had the oddest sensation that I felt—*wings*.

"By the time I looked up again, my mother-in-law's face was red and swollen from lack of air. I vaguely remember telling my husband to respect his mother and not to kill her, then with a strength I wasn't aware I had, I shoved him ten feet out of the hall and well inside our bedroom.

"I locked the bedroom door. Again I knew I was not alone. The heavenly calm that this presence gave me succeeded in penetrating my husband's anger, and he cooled off as well.

"After the situation was defused, I began to tremble uncontrollably. Not from fear but because I knew that there had been a Presence in that hall even greater than the angels that had protected me. For weeks I couldn't stop praising God for his overwhelming love and caring. I also know today that God loves and protects my beautiful little daughter—as he has since before she was born."

Beth Westmoreland—Which Way Is Up?

Beth Westmoreland of North Carolina had an encounter when she was very young, but today she still remembers every detail with amazing clarity:

"When I was around six or seven years old, my family went on vacation to the ocean along the South Carolina shore. My older sister, who was seventeen, was told to watch me on the beach while my parents made lunch back in our trailer.

"This section of the beach was deserted and certainly

no fun for a teenage girl, so my sister warned me to stay put and then left for a walk down the beach. Being headstrong, too sure of myself, and indignant that my sister thought she could tell me what to do, I waited until she was out of sight, then galloped straight into the water.

"I'd known how to swim in pools for years and didn't know enough to be afraid of the ocean. The waters that day were turbulent. Before I knew it, a huge wave knocked me down and the undertow grabbed me and began pulling me out to sea.

"The waves were so rough and sandy that I couldn't even get my bearings as to which way was up. It felt as if I was underwater forever. I refused to give up and fought and struggled to find any indication of which way to go to find air.

"Suddenly, I saw golden rays from the sun slice through the water right in front of me—where they illumined *legs!*—big, 'man' legs, with big feet. I grabbed them and held on tight. The man scooped me up out of the water as easily as if I were a baby in a swing. I'll never forget how strong his arms felt, or how he looked. He was real big, and he had a big black beard, thick black hair, and lots of chest hair. My dad has red hair and freckles, and no hair on his legs, and I'd never seen a man that big or that hairy.

"The man carried me to my blanket, wrapped me in a towel, and without a word he walked away. I looked around for my sister, mom, dad, or anybody. When I looked back toward the direction the man had walked, he was gone. He'd just disappeared.

"The towel wasn't mine. It had pink and blue shells and fishes printed on it. I was exhausted, but I ran as fast as I could back to the trailer. I tried to tell my parents what had happened, but I don't think they put much stock in my story. Maybe it was too farfetched for them. "After lunch that day, I went back to the blanket. There was no towel with shells and fishes. There were my footprints and my sister's but no 'big man' footprints. Not anywhere. But years later I still remember every inch of that brawny, dark-haired stranger, and I remember the odd sensation of feeling no heavier than a feather in his arms. Of course he left me something to remember him by—my life.

"So if anyone tries to tell you that all angels are blond with white gowns, surrounded in light, I beg to differ!"

Nicholas Poliansky—the Basketball Game

Hope Poliansky describes how, in October 1992, her son Nicholas was playing basketball with his friend Danny in Danny's backyard. Hope and Danny's mother, although members of different denominations, share a strong Christian faith. That day, in the midst of playing basketball, Nicholas stepped too far back away from the court and landed on a temporary cover over the deep end of the in-ground swimming pool. To the horror of Danny's mother, who was standing nearby, the cover was not well-secured. She could only watch helplessly as it gave way under the weight of the boy's body.

At first Nicholas slipped and slid, desperately trying to find a foothold where there was none. But then, suddenly, and in full view of everyone watching, he was lifted and carried off the cover and out of danger. That day as Danny's mother recounted the incident, she told the Polianskys with absolute certainty that Nicholas was carried by an angel. There simply was no other explanation.

Kathryn Butcher—the Halloween Prank

Kathryn Butcher of Ann Arbor, Michigan, has never forgotten a Halloween prank she played as a college student in 1958. She and some of her high-spirited girlfriends decided to "toilet paper" the trees in the yards of the college fraternities. At one house, however, the girls were discovered in the midst of their prank. They all made a run for it, with Kathryn in the lead.

As Kathryn tells it, "In fear, I led the pack and leaped over a fence into—nothingness! In their backyard someone had dug an enormous hole, which in the dark had been impossible to see." But in the midst of the fall, "I felt myself lifted in mid-air and carried across the opening to the bank on the other side. I was astonished." She quickly turned to yell a warning to her friends, but no one was anywhere near her. She knew then that she'd been saved by an angel.

For Kathryn, the evening that had started with a college prank ended with her feeling protected and loved—a feeling so strong that she still carries it with her even decades later.

Candace Hanable—the Red Pick-up

Candace Hanable of Lancaster, California, is married now and a mother, but she'll never forget washing her red truck one day when she was nineteen years old. It was a 4 x 4, and high off the ground. The truck was parked on an incline, and she had a hard time reaching the top of the cab. As she climbed onto the roof from the bed of the truck, she lost her footing and fell backward toward the ground.

During the fall, everything seemed to go into slow motion—slow enough for her to know that she was falling bottom-first and was about to land on her spinal column. The last things she saw before impact were her feet in front of her face.

But today Karen recounts with amazement: "When I landed, I was on my feet. I couldn't believe it when I found myself standing. I had *seen* my feet in front of my face. An angel must have caught me and helped me land. There was no possible way I could have fallen the way I did and landed feet first and uninjured!"

Bette Fetters—the Well

Perhaps our favorite story of angels' breaking a fall comes from Bette Fetters, who now lives in Ohio. We'll let her tell it in her own words.

"As a small child I was adopted to work on a farm. The couple who adopted me were troubled and unable to love and comfort because they were lost in their own cycle of violence.

"One day in early September of the year I was twelve, they left for a few weeks' visit with out-of-state relatives. It was my responsibility to care for the livestock before catching my school bus. However, one morning the pump at the barn would not produce the needed water.

"Doing what I'd seen them do many times, I searched for a bucket and rope to bring up water from the well. All I could find were an oversized bucket and a comparatively new rope. I pushed the boards off the well, which opened on the ground next to the barn pump. Holding tightly to the rope, I lowered it carefully, trying to keep the rope from even getting wet.

"Unfortunately, the water level was so low, I couldn't keep control of the bucket. As it hit the water, it began immediately to fill with water, the weight of which began pulling me into the well. I was old enough to know I had two choices—let go of the rope and bucket, or be dragged into the well. I knew one thing for certain—my adopted father would kill me if I lost that new rope. So the decision was made—better to fall into the well. At least they would know that I died trying.

"As I reached the mouth of the well, I heard an actual audible voice. It commanded: Lie down on your stomach. I remember thinking, nonsensically, *I can't lie down, I'm falling into the well.* As I lurched to the mouth of the well, I heard once more the audible voice, repeating the same words. But now it was too late—I was falling. There was no time to think anything; I was just expecting to feel the icy water.

"Then, as I expected to splash, unseen arms caught me, bore me up, and laid me on my stomach by the side of the well. Stunned by what had happened, I looked all around wondering who had spoken to me, who had saved me from my fall.

"Seeing no one, I reasoned, *It must be God!* As that thought came, so, too, there was a warmth that flooded my being, and I knew at that moment that I was loved. It was a revelation that I had never experienced before, as I had always felt unloved and unwanted.

"Though nothing changed between me and the couple on their return, I now knew that the God I had heard about oh-so-fleetingly from a friend, must be real. Now, when there was a need to hide from the anger, I talked to him and found comfort and guidance there. It was many years before I heard of guardian angels, but when I did, I knew that my angel had been there when needed and had spared my life."

Once again, we find an example of an angelic encounter that not only saved from physical harm but brought a sure, life-changing knowledge of God's love and grace.

Intervening Angels

The Gospels tell how an angel of the Lord appeared to Joseph to warn him to flee to Egypt with Mary and young Jesus to escape the murderous wrath of King Herod. Angels have appeared throughout history to avert disaster. That they still do so today seems clear from the following story.

Margaret Medford and the Dobermans

It was about a mile from Margaret's house to the dentist's office, and since it was a nice day she decided to walk to her appointment. The office was in a shopping center located at the intersection of a busy five-way downtown boulevard.

Just as Margaret got to the rise of a knoll at the end of the residential part of the street adjoining the shopping center, two snarling Doberman pinschers charged out of their front yard. They sandwiched Margaret between them and edged forward in an attack posture.

Margaret, knowing the danger she was in, tried to remain passive and do nothing to further provoke the animals' attack, but they continued to advance. She expected to be knocked down and bitten at any moment.

Traffic from the opposing lanes was thick, but car after car passed without noticing Margaret's predicament.

Suddenly a young man leaped from a shiny black pick-up truck that appeared showroom-new. He strode through the traffic and took immediate command of the situation. With a word and a gesture he broke up the melee and sent the dogs yelping back to their yard. He then turned and walked straight through traffic back to his truck.

Margaret was momentarily stunned by the total

authority shown by the mysterious stranger, and, noticing that he had paused to make a left turn into the parking lot, she hurried to catch up with him. She wanted to thank him at least, maybe offer him a tip.

She saw him turn, but when she got to the spot where both she and the driver should have arrived simultaneously, there was nothing—absolutely no sign of any person or truck. The young man and the shiny black truck had vanished without a trace.

Chapter
5

Guardian Angel Rescuers

Tractors, Trucks, and Automobiles

Guardian angels, it seems, have no trouble at all with modern conveniences such as cars, trucks, or even farm tractors, as we see from the following stories, which range from the simple to the dramatic.

Evelyn Yankle—Out of Harm's Way

Evelyn tells two stories of being saved from a traffic-related injury:

"When I was eighteen years old, I was working for Michigan Bell Telephone in Flint. One Friday on my lunch hour, I was about to cross a busy street. The light was green, and I stepped out into the street when I was gently held back by a strong pressure on my shoulder. At that moment, a large bus, previously unseen, zoomed in front of me, exactly where I would have been standing if I'd taken even a step or two. When I looked behind me to thank the person who had saved me, I was completely alone.

"Then, a couple of years ago, I was driving my car. The light turned green, and I started forward. Suddenly my car, which was in perfect working condition, came to a dead stop just as an eighteen-wheeler ran the red light and barreled through the intersection!

"I wouldn't be here today if my guardian angel hadn't stopped the car. Isn't our dear Lord wonderful in the way he cares for us?"

From the Perils That Fly by Day

Judith Rowsey of Tampa is convinced that God has assigned guardian angels to her car because she does not like driving and needs their protection because of her poor driving skills. She would be aware of their presence when she was alone or in a dangerous situation. A few years ago Judith and her nine-year-old daughter were driving about five miles in Oklahoma City to pick up a new pair of glasses. The winds were very high that day, and there were a number of construction vehicles on the road.

Judith looked up and saw a flatbed truck loaded with 4 x 8-foot plywood boards. Judith was going west, and the truck was going east in the other lane, coming toward her. Suddenly a strong gust of wind picked up three of the sheets of plywood and blew them off the truck.

The boards flew through the air straight for Judith's car. The first board headed right for her windshield at an angle that would break the windshield and decapitate the occupants of the car. Her daughter screamed, raised her knees up to her chest, and instinctively tried to shield her face. Judith had time only to pray, "Father!" That one-word prayer was a prayer of faith, calling on the name of the God she loved and trusted.

It was then that Judith saw the angel—at the front of her car. He looked like a clean-cut, boy-next-door football player . . . only larger and very muscular. He looked right into Judith's eyes with a knowing smile, almost as a human would do if he winked. There was an instantaneous communication between the angel and the driver, not in words but heart-to-heart. Then the angel put his hand up and skillfully deflected the first board. Next, with the skill of a basketball player blocking a shot, he knocked the second board over to the side of the road. The third board came toward the roof of the car. The angel tapped it. The board made a small dent in the roof of the car before sailing to the shoulder of the highway.

Judith said, "Did you see that?"

"What?" asked her daughter, still visibly shaken.

"That angel? Did you see the angel?"

She said, "No, I didn't."

"It was so thrilling," Judith explained. "You saw those plywood boards coming towards us. I prayed, 'Father!' and he sent his angel. The Scriptures say, 'I bless my people because they know my name.' I knew his name, and I used it. Praise God—he preserved our lives!"

Karen Martin—the Minivan

It was a happy day for Karen Martin of Austin, Texas. She and her husband had purchased a brand-new truck and were going to pick it up. Karen was driving her minivan, and her husband, Don, was in the passenger seat when they stopped at a red light at the corner of Congress and Stassney. To Karen's horror, she looked up to find a large station wagon turning from the far right lane and heading for her van, head-on, at forty to forty-five miles per hour. There was no way the Martins could move. Karen recalls, "Only when the other driver was twelve feet in front of me did she even use her brakes!"

Just before impact, Karen saw a strange sight—"Someone," in white light, was standing in front of her van. The white silhouette vanished as the two vehicles collided.

Although the collision was head-on and the station wagon was totaled, there were no injuries in either car— and the Martins' minivan needed no repairs other than a new bumper!

Karen says, "The only way I can explain what happened is the presence of a guardian angel!"

Sam Johnston—Stopped in Time

Sam Johnston tells of when his father had a job transfer from one area of the country to another. The family managed to pack everything they owned into a trailer, which they bolted to their car.

Sam's mother took the first driving shift. She drove faster than she should have and was stopped by an officer, who pulled her over and gave her a kind warning to slow down.

Sam's parents traded places while they were pulled over. Perhaps a minute after their start-up, a tire came off the car! The car was still going slowly enough for Sam's dad to be able to bring the car and trailer to a safe stop.

All of them sat stunned, only guessing what would have happened if they had been still going seventy miles per hour. The family immediately looked back to thank the officer—but he was gone. He wasn't on the road behind them, and there was no way he could have crossed the median. He had simply disappeared.

Charles Ward—Night Drive

Vesta Ward's brother is a courier for the telephone company. They tell this story:

VESTA: "My brother Charles drives a truck at night, delivering mail and supplies to central offices and construction sites along a two-hundred-mile route in Illinois. He enjoys driving at night, as it gives him time to pray and think. I often awaken in the night and pray for his safety because his route is over a narrow, winding road with dangerous drop-offs along the side."

CHARLES: "One night in 1989, I was driving my telephone utility truck along Route 127. Feeling unusually drowsy, I reminded myself out loud to 'stay awake.' The next thing I knew, however, I felt an obvious but gentle touch on my sleeve, rousing me from sleep.

"I awakened to realize I was at the edge of a three-foot drop-off beside a rock wall. It was too late to do anything. The front tires were already over the edge, hurtling me forward to impact.

"Then suddenly, I knew with great surety exactly what to do. I calmly turned the steering wheel slightly to the left, and the truck was back on solid ground, coming to a gentle stop. I was safe!

"A feeling of relief, thanksgiving, and wonder flooded over me. Who had touched me? How had I known exactly how to save the truck that had been beyond saving?

"In my heart I knew the answer. Still, I searched the truck for anything at all that could have touched and awakened me.

There was nothing—nothing *visible*, I should say. Yet I now know for certain that *someone* rides with me at night, and I am grateful."

Wynter Rowe—Angels in Winter

In January of 1990, fourteen-year-old Wynter Rowe couldn't resist hitching a ride with her mother, Linda, who was going to pick up some ordered supplies thirty miles away at a mall. Linda warned Wynter that it would have to be a quick in and out because of the dangerous weather moving into their part of Oregon.

When they left the mall at 5:30, snow clouds had already darkened the sky prematurely. Freezing rain and snow were forecast, and the radio warned that there was already "black ice"—which was impossible to see—on the roads.

Linda held the Lincoln well within the speed limit on Interstate 5. "The pavement seems pretty dry," she said. "Hopefully, we'll get past Blackwell Hill before the freeze and snowfall." Blackwell Hill was known for being treacherous when icy.

Falling into a familiar ritual, mother and daughter began singing to pass the time: "You've got to love the Lord your God with all your heart, and all your soul and all your mind, and love mankind, as you would yourself . . ."

They were just yards from Blackwell Hill and well into the third verse when, as Wynter says, "Suddenly it felt as though I no longer had a seat under me. I saw Mom gasp in surprise as the car fishtailed wildly to the left. She let up on the accelerator and lightly tapped the brakes, then released them and tried tapping them again. The wheels couldn't get a hold, and the rear end of the car skewed in the opposite direction."

"We're losing it," Linda cried. "Hold on. Oh, God— help us!"

Now out of control, the car performed two perfect doughnuts before sliding—backward—into the right-hand lane and up the hill.

Wynter continues: "I began to black out but at the last moment looked upward—directly into the eyes of an angel sitting overhead. I turned and looked at Mom, who was trying desperately to bring the car under control— and I saw another angel covering her hands with his.

"I saw Mom's lips moving in silent prayer—and I prayed, too." By this time the car was shooting across the lanes of traffic, barely missing one vehicle only to be thrown into the path of another—yet missing that one, too. The car nosed over the right-hand embankment, teetered there for a moment, then double-looped back across the highway into the left-hand lane.

Wynter then saw her mother's eyes widen in terror, and she looked in the same direction. "To my horror," she says, "I saw the dividing guardrail just a few feet in front of our speeding car. I looked imploringly at the angel above me, and felt him silently prompting me to call out—as I did—'Jesus! Please help us!'"

She heard her mother say, "We're going through!" Then she scrunched her eyes shut for the moment of impact.

But the impact never came. "I was aware of a forever silence. There was no grinding, crashing, or ripping. No shattered glass driving into me. And no pain! I wondered if I was in heaven.

"Confused, I opened one eye and found that we were parked safely off the road by the guardrail. The engine was quiet, but there seemed to be no damage to the car."

After the police came, after the Rowes were calm, the car was turned around, and the rest of the drive was made in safety through the snow that had finally started to fall. Once they were home and soothed by mugs of hot chocolate, the two were finally calm enough to compare notes.

"You know," Linda told Wynter, "as we headed for the guardrail, all I could do was hold on to the steering wheel. Somehow I *knew* that's what God wanted me to do. In the last split second before we hit, I asked God to take me and spare you. I didn't want you to suffer. I'd done all I could and felt that the end was at hand. Then I heard you cry out your simple prayer.

"When you did, God showed me six gigantic angels, with their hands interlocked, blocking the guardrail. They diverted our car."

She had also experienced the same two angels inside

the car that Wynter had seen. With awe, Linda explained, "The angel next to me parked the car, turned it off, and set the brake, while the other shielded Wynter."

To this day, neither has forgotten a moment of their ride—nor have they forgotten the six angels, all in a row. Or, as perhaps should be said, "Six angels, all for two Rowes."

David Lee and the Tractor

A couple of years ago, Tina Lee's husband, David, was clearing some land to enlarge their produce garden near their home in rural Georgia. The Lees enjoy gardening, and their crops of peas, butterbeans, tomatoes, and potatoes (among other things) fed them year 'round. As David drove the tractor, Tina went inside to answer the telephone, which was by a window from which she could watch both her husband and their two-year-old son Joshua, who was playing near the house.

As she picked up the phone, she was horrified to look outside and see David on the ground—and the tractor on top of him.

"Joshua, stay right there!" she yelled to her son as she raced past him to try to save her husband.

Tina arrived to find the tractor pinning David—by the rubber sole of his work boot. The ignition key was turned halfway to off, which had stalled the large tractor. Tina immediately climbed up and turned off the motor, then she helped David out from under the tractor, and together they were able to right it. The worst injury he suffered was a twisted ankle.

As they discussed the accident, David shook his head and said he didn't understand what had happened: He remembered the tractor's being right over him—then moving away from him as if someone had shoved it aside. He also had no idea why the engine had stalled when it did. He had expected to lose his leg if not his life.

Just then little Joshua came running over to his parents.

"Did you see him, Daddy?" Joshua asked.

"Who?" asked David.

"The man," the little boy said, his eyes still wide. "He was as tall as the trees! He moved the tractor when it was falling on Daddy, then he turned the key."

Tina and David hadn't seen, but they both knew that "from the mouths of babes" had come the only explanation for what had happened. "I've always believed in angels and felt their comfort," says Tina, "but this solidified my belief that angels are always protecting us, too!"

Fire!

The book of Daniel relates the dramatic account of three men—Shadrach, Meshach, and Abednego—who refused to worship an idol of gold. When King Nebuchadnezzar threatened to throw them alive into a fiery furnace if they did not worship the idol instead of Jehovah, they calmly replied: "If we are thrown into the blazing furnace, the God we serve is able to save us from it, and he will rescue us from your hand, O king. But even if he does not, we want you to know, O king, that we will not serve your gods or worship the image of gold you have set up."

This angered Nebuchadnezzar so greatly that he had the three men tied up. Then he had the furnace stoked so that it burned seven times hotter than usual—the heat was so intense, the Bible tells us, that the soldiers who threw the bound men into the furnace died from the heat.

Once they were thrown into the furnace, according to Daniel, chapter 3, "King Nebuchadnezzar leaped to his feet in amazement and asked his advisers, 'Weren't there three men that we tied up and threw into the fire?' They replied, 'Certainly, O king.' He said, 'Look! I see four men walking around in the fire, unbound and unharmed, and the fourth looks like a son of the gods.'"

So the king summoned the three men out of the furnace, and they walked out without as much as a singe on their clothing, or the smell of smoke anywhere on them.

Then Nebuchadnezzar said, "Praise be to the God of Shadrach, Meshach and Abednego, who has sent his angel and rescued his servants!"

He then commanded that their God be respected— and gave the three men positions of great importance in the land.

From the following accounts, it's clear that God uses angels in the same way (although perhaps a bit less dramatically) today.

Paula Ratcliff—Electric Blanket

Paula Ratcliff, who currently lives in Washington State with her husband, tells this story.

"About four years ago, my husband's grandmother gave us an electric blanket that she no longer used. We couldn't wait to use it and plugged it in right away when it was time for bed.

"That night I heard my name spoken softly, without alarm, over and over again. When I finally awoke I saw a veiled-like, white vaporous figure standing by my bed. I sat straight up and noticed sparks lying at the foot of the bed. The blanket had an electrical short in it and was ready to catch fire!

"I awakened my husband, and as he sat up in bed we both saw our angel go straight up, move over the top of our bed, and go right through the wall. The memory of our angelic visitor remains as real and vivid to both of us today as it was that very night!"

Roy K. Hendricks—the Oil Heater

Roy Hendricks bought a new K-oil heater in October 1984, satisfied that he'd be ready for winter. In fact, it worked well and kept his mobile home toasty as the weather turned cold.

The temperature during the night of December 23 of that year was in the twenties, so Roy decided to keep the heater on all night, as he had many times since he bought it.

About 3:00 A.M., he was sleeping, face to the wall, when, as he tells it: "I heard my name, Roy, called three times. I said: 'What do you want?' and rolled over. The first thing I saw was flames up to the ceiling—and what appeared to be the outline of a person between me and the fire."

He got up, grabbed the nearby fuel tank, and threw it clear of the fire, out into the yard. Then he ran outside and asked his neighbor to call the fire department. When he went back inside, there was dense smoke but no sign of fire. After things calmed down and the mobile home aired out, he was able to go back to bed.

Roy concludes by saying that the next morning there weren't even black spots on the ceiling, although he'd seen eight-foot flames with his own eyes. When he told people about the voice, the figure, and the flames, some people thought he was loony. But then he shows them what may seem an odd reminder of God's love: his K-oil heater, burned, warped, and blackened to a crisp.

Lorraine Buckles and the Car Battery

Lorraine Buckles of Florida told us this story: "About thirty years ago, I was a long-distance telephone operator for Southern Bell Telephone company in Daytona Beach, Florida. At the time, I worked the 2:30 to 10:30 P.M. shift. This particular night I got off work at ten. My old car, which had battery problems, was parked in front of the Southern Bell building on Highway U.S. 1. Someone had told me that if I would keep putting water in the battery, it would keep working and save me from having to buy a new one. I liked the idea, since money was scarce in those days."

That night was warm and absolutely still. Unfortunately, Lorraine's car did not start. She got out, raised the hood, and removed the battery caps. She then struck a match and leaned over to look into the open cells.

As soon as she bent over, a puff of air blew the match out. Surprised, since there was no air moving whatsoever, she looked at nearby bushes and trees, but nothing was stirring in the least. Besides, she was sure it wasn't a stream of wind—it had been a specific puff from right over her shoulder. Puzzled, she tore off a second match, but as she went to light it, she heard the command, "Don't." She got the message and lit no more matches.

Says Lorraine, "When I finally got the car to a service station and explained to the mechanic what I'd done, he told me that I had done a very dangerous thing, because open batteries, if ignited, can easily explode. I believe an angel saved me. What else?"

Paula Stewart

Another audible angel encounter was experienced by Paula Stewart.

In 1975 Paula had just moved to Salem, Oregon, and

had found a nice living situation with a roommate named Virginia. The two young women worked together on the swing shift as dorm matrons at a boarding school for Native American teenagers. On January 8, they finished their shift, making certain that their charges were in bed, and came home. Because it was Virginia's birthday, they decided to relax and have a snack in front of the fireplace. After they had eaten, the fire had died down, and as bedtime approached, both young women began to fcel woozy and lightheaded. Soon neither of them was able to think clearly, and the situation soon became more extreme. From the floor where she lay, Virginia whispered to Paula that she couldn't move and was losing consciousness.

Paula realized that she, too, was about to pass out. *This is so strange!* she thought. *What's wrong with us? Was it something we ate?* When Virginia passed out, Paula tried not to panic. Unable to get up from the floor and very afraid, she began to pray.

Then she heard an audible voice say loudly and clearly, "Go outside. Breathe fresh air." She heard the message repeated three times. Much to her surprise, she felt herself being forcibly dragged outside by an unseen hand.

Once outside she again collapsed, but soon her vertigo slowed down and she began to feel more clear-headed. She realized that she had to get her roommate outside, so as soon as she could stand, she went back in. Virginia was woozy but awake, and Paula was able to get her outside. The girls sat in the snow until their heads began to clear. They called Virginia's sister, who came and got them and took them to the emergency ward of the local hospital.

At the hospital, when they described what had happened, doctors pinpointed the problem. The Presto logs they'd used for the fire weren't completely burned out. When they closed the damper to go to bed, the logs created carbon monoxide, which was then recirculated through the house's heating system. Both girls' blood was filled with carbon monoxide, which took several months to clear out completely.

Paula concludes, without hesitation, that if it hadn't been for the voice and the unseen Presence, she wouldn't be here today. "Oh, yeah," she says, "I definitely believe in angels!"

The Fire and Misty, Boots, Baby Baby, and Little Bits

God cares about animals! Jesus himself said that not even a sparrow falls to earth without God noticing. The next story of angelic intervention proves this point again.

Maureen Broadbent and her husband had a home in the countryside outside of Corona in Southern California. One memorable day, Maureen returned from grocery shopping to find her house in flames. The volunteer fire department was already on the scene but just standing by, watching the fire progress.

"We can't go near it," explained the chief. "It sounds like there's fireworks going off inside the house."

Maureen realized that the popping noises coming from inside the house were from the guns her husband kept to keep coyotes at bay. They were firing in the heat.

Maureen heard barking and realized that their two dogs, Misty and Boots, their two cats, Baby Baby and Little Bits, as well as the visiting neighbor dog, had escaped through the doggie door into the backyard. Also, because of coyotes in this still-wild section of Southern California, the backyard was surrounded by a heavy-duty, eight-foot-high chain-link fence with barbed wire wound on top. Maureen started toward the gate to release the animals, but the fire warden held her back and pointed to the top of the fence. Somehow the fire had downed overhead wires. "We can't tell if they're phone wires or electrical wires. If they're electric, that whole fence will be alive. No one can touch it."

Maureen was grieved by the burning of her house and possessions, but she couldn't stand the thought of the swiftly spreading fire's killing her pets trapped in the backyard. She ran around to the back and talked to the dogs, Misty and Boots, and cats Baby and Little Bits. They were frightened but trusting, mutely begging for her to help them escape the escalating heat. But the situation seemed hopeless.

Maureen sank to the ground, crying, and began to pray: "Oh God, how do I get my animals out of here? I'm afraid to touch the fence . . ."

Suddenly her attention was caught by the figure of a man running through the wild acres that surrounded the house. Although the brush and bristles were thick and waist high, the man was shirtless and running with ease. Maureen knew everyone who lived in this remote area, but she'd never seen this man before. As he approached, she saw that he was about six feet tall, blond-haired and blue-eyed. Although he ran with effortless speed, when he burst from the thorny brush she saw that he was barefoot.

Without saying a word, he went to the fence, grabbed it, and easily *pulled it up from the bottom* until there was an opening large enough for the cats, the border collie, the neighbor's dog, and even the German shepherd to squeeze through. The animals escaped at once and surrounded Maureen where she sat on the ground.

There she was smothered with licks and sloppy kisses, in the center of a joyful reunion.

When she looked up to thank the mysterious stranger, he wasn't there. In fact, he wasn't anywhere. From the Broadbents' home, she could see for miles in every direction, and besides the firemen, there was no one either at the house or heading through the fields.

As a postscript, the Broadbents add that no human, no matter how large or well-muscled, could move the fence back down to where it had been so easily lifted up.

The Broadbents now live in Texas, where Maureen happily reports she is now aware of God's love and the protection of his angels on a daily basis.

The Mystery Doorbell

It was a normal August day for the family of Bill and Mary Ann Wittlieff of southwestern Michigan. Their oldest son was at work, but the three elementary-school-age children were in the living room with their visiting cousin, happily playing video games. Bill was in the kitchen. Suddenly the doorbell rang at the back door. The Wittlief's home is out in the country, and "drop-in" guests are unusual. Brent, their second-oldest son, went and answered the door, but no one was there.

No sooner had he opened and closed the back door than the front doorbell rang. From where he stood in the kitchen, Bill could see out the picture window at the front of the house—and he could see that no one was there. In fact, no one was anywhere around the house.

"What's wrong with the doorbell?" Bill asked himself out loud. "Brent, buzz the back bell."

Brent opened the back door and pushed the bell. This time there was no sound at all.

"I'd better go down and check the transformer," said

Bill. Everything seemed normal as he went down the basement stairs.

But he opened the door—and found that the whole basement was on fire! He quickly got the kids out of the house and called the fire department. Not long after, the living room floor, on which the children had been sitting, collapsed in flames.

The Wittlieffs lost everything in the house in that consuming fire. Could it be that the fire melted the wires, causing a short that rang the doorbell? If so, was this a coincidence . . . or was it a warning from God?

As for Mary Ann, she is certain that angels rang the doorbells to warn the family of the hidden fire they could neither feel nor see.

Chapter
6

But Where Was My Guardian Angel?

It is exciting to read the eyewitness accounts of people who have been saved by their guardian angels. God does work in marvelous ways. Nothing is too hard for God and his angels!

While we thank God for the gracious watchcare of the angels, there are also times when the angels do not intervene. Accidents happen, and good people are hurt or even killed. Where are the guardian angels then?

They are there all the time! More often than we realize they are doing their unseen work, guiding, helping and protecting us. Sometimes they intervene miraculously.

What would life be like if they always kept us from accidents? What a strange world it would be if everyone could drive like a maniac but there would never be a dented fender. It would certainly be a different world from the world we know if angels would always catch us when we tripped, and no one would fall accidentally.

When God in his infinite wisdom created our world, he created the laws of nature as well. And the laws of nature, including gravity, speed, and motion, are good laws. It is seldom that God chooses to override his own laws, and then only for reasons of his own.

We have searched, but we have not been able to find the pattern that explains why God at times has his angels intervene and at other times does not. The angelic help may come to a strong believer living a godly life. Some are nonbelievers when they are touched by the angels' ministry. Often it leads them to a faith in God, but sometimes it does not. The Bible teaches that God sends his rain on the just and the unjust alike. God is sovereign, and for reasons of his own may have his angels help the unjust. He is not obligated to explain to us why he chooses to have his angelic hosts help one person and not another; or to rescue in one circumstance but not in another.

This chapter is not long enough, and its authors are not wise enough to answer the problem of pain and evil in the universe. We do know that the angel of the Lord encamps around those who fear him (Psalm 34:7). We also know that in all things God works for the good of those who love him (Romans 8:28).

The book of Job teaches that when pain and suffering happen in our physical lives, there may be things going on in the spiritual realm that we never know. It is likely that when we encounter problems, pain, and heartache that our good angels are active in ways that we do not observe. Our angels may be present and active and limit the extent of an accident. In another chapter we will explain how angels strengthen and support us in difficult times. In the Garden of Gethsemane an angel ministered to Jesus. He did not save him from the agony of the cross, but his ministry was a part of the heavenly Father's gracious provision to help Jesus endure the suffering he faced. God's angels may play a part in helping us become more Christlike in times of adversity.

Before a television taping, one woman asked Joan Wester Anderson, the author of *Where Angels Walk*, "Where were the guardian angels when my daughter was stabbed to death?"

Joan answered, "I believe they may have been with her, taking away the pain after the first wound." It could well be!

Katherine Lippy wrote us from Hagerstown, Maryland: "My little nine-year-old friend Jason was hit by a car and killed. His mother and I are good friends. Well, last spring I was sitting painting a ceramic angel. All of a sudden Jason came to mind, and I spoke my thoughts out loud, 'Lord, where was Jason's guardian angel that day?' (like he has to tell me!!!)

"My all-too-human questioning brought an instant answer as I heard him speak, 'Carrying Jason into my bosom.' I certainly could see angels swooping Jason up— instantly as the car hit him—he didn't even feel a pain—he just went to be with Jesus. Praise God, angels are ever present."

Chapter
7

Was It a Coincidence?
An Angel? Or God?

Monica was heartbroken. From the beginning she had prayed for her son, lovingly taught him the faith, and tried always to be a Christian example. But her son, Augustine, went through a terrible teenage rebellion that continued into his young adult years. He lived a self-centered life, constantly seeking pleasure of all kinds, especially sexual enjoyment.

One day in the garden he heard a voice saying, "Take and read." It seemed to Augustine that the voice was speaking directly to him. He took it to mean that he should take the Bible and read it. He did, and was converted. Augustine made a complete change in his life, dedicated himself to Jesus Christ, and became a leader in the church. His writings have influenced Christianity for over fifteen hundred years.

All this happened because of the voice that said: "Take and read." Where did this voice come from? Was it a person that Augustine just happened to overhear? Was it the Holy Spirit at work in his life? Was it his guardian angel sent on a special mission from God?

When a person has an experience that may be an encounter with an angel, often the question comes up, "Was this just a coincidence? Was it an angel? Or was it God?"

It is a good question that has been asked for ages. Let's try to give some insight and some guidelines.

Sometimes it is clearly an angel. In Luke 1:26 where it

says "God sent the angel Gabriel" to Mary, there is no doubt that it was an angel. When a person today sees an angel in a form that is unmistakably supernatural, that person is certain that it is an angel. But if the angel appears in human form, as angels often did in the Bible, how can one know? And can one know if something happens even though no one or nothing is seen?

In several stories in this book, the persons relating their experience believe that the "person" they met was an angel. The evidence given the most for this is that the person appeared from nowhere, disappeared, or both. For example, in Bill Henry's story, a man suddenly appeared on the cowcatcher of his speeding locomotive. An ordinary mortal would have been killed in an attempt to board a train in such a way. At the end of the account, when they looked for the mysterious flagman, no one was there.

It would seem to be a safe rule that when a person appears in a way that defies our usual explanation and performs some act or service usually associated with angels, it is an angel. That is also the simplest explanation.

At other times, individuals have been helped by someone who appeared to belong in that setting. Yet when they tried to locate the person who had been their helper, they discovered that there had been no one present who fit that description.

These mysterious people are probably angels. One cannot be certain, but it does seem to be the best explanation. The authors would not be dogmatic about any one occurrence, but since we have received so many reports of this kind we are convinced that angels do appear in this way. We believe they may purposely appear as a person but choose a form (including color of hair, size, with or without glasses, and so on) so that no one else in that setting has a clue that this was an angel encounter.

But what about strangers—who come in a normal way, give words of encouragement, or perform a mission of mercy, and then leave in a perfectly ordinary manner? One cannot state with certainty that an angel was present. It could be coincidental—that someone was passing by just when needed. Some people believe there are no coincidences—that everything is ordered by God. Others believe that some things do happen by chance. Regardless of one's theology on this point, it could also be that God in his mercy used a human to meet the need. If God was behind it, he is to be thanked whether the ministry was done by humans or by angels.

There is good reason to believe that many times these strangers are actually angels. There are examples in the Bible of angels having appeared in human form. The writer to the Hebrews thought this happened often enough to admonish: "Do not forget to entertain strangers, for by so doing some people have entertained angels without knowing it" (Hebrews 13:2).

How can you be certain that such a stranger is an angel? You can't! And it really doesn't matter if God meets your need through a person or an angel. If it were important for you to know, the good Lord would certainly give you a clue. But to be safe follow the teaching of the Scripture and treat each stranger as though that individual is an angel. The implication of the Bible is that more often than we suspect, angels do walk among us in the form of humans. You can add excitement to your life if you are always anticipating that the next person you meet may be an angel in disguise. It's also fun to look back and wonder if you have met any angels on assignment today. That can be a practical part of faith: expecting God to be at work.

We asked a friend, "Have you had any experiences with angels?"

She answered, somewhat reprovingly, "No, but I have had many experiences with the Holy Spirit."

We understood her gentle rebuke. She was certain that God was active in her life and did not want anyone giving credit to an angel for what God was doing, attributing every act of Providence directly to God. Others I know see their guardian angel at work in everything. Which perception is correct?

It must be said from the outset that God is free to do what he knows is best. If he wants to work directly in someone's life, that's his prerogative. It's also his choice if he wants to work through an angel. Perhaps some of our confusion is owing to the fact that God may choose to work directly with one person and sometimes through angels with another.

For example, if we are given a message, how do we know if it is from God or from an angel? It's easy if the message includes some identification of the speaker, such as, "I am Gabriel, the angel of the Lord." Most often this is not the case. Rather the message is given usually without words that are heard, without identifying the speaker as God or an angel. From the Bible we know that God does speak in both ways. We also know that angels never seek credit for what they do. In fact, angels characteristically do not wait around to be thanked. Perhaps one reason for there being so many stories of angels disappearing right after their work is done is to direct the thanks and the glory to God.

Again, when there is no way of knowing if it is an angel or God, one may speculate about how God works but realize that whichever one it is, it is still God. If it is important for us to know how God chooses to work in our lives, he will let us know.

Sometimes in the Bible, angels are clearly angels. At other times the angel is identified with God. This is the case with the Old Testament use of "the angel of the Lord." Many believe that the angel of the Lord was Jesus Christ, coming to earth in a visible form before the Incarnation. Here is some evidence to support that view.

In the Bible there are times when the angel of the Lord turns out to be none other than God himself. When Hagar ran away from Sarah, the angel of the LORD found her. The angel of the LORD promised to do himself what only God can do (Genesis 16:10–12). The account continues in verse 13: "She gave this name to the LORD who spoke to her: 'You are the God who sees me.'" The "angel of the LORD" and the "LORD" (Yaweh or Jehovah) are clearly one and the same.

When this angel appeared to Moses in the well-known account of the burning bush, "the angel of the LORD appeared to him in flames of fire from within a bush" (Exodus 3:2). Two verses later it says, "God called to him from within the bush." Here and other places in the Old Testament the words for "God" and "the angel of the LORD" are used interchangeably.

Yet the angel of the LORD is separate from God. In Zechariah (and elsewhere) the angel of the LORD talks to the LORD Almighty. How can the angel of the LORD be God and be separate from God at the same time? This mystery can be understood if we recognize it as being similar to Christ in his earthly life: being truly God, yet being separate from God. So we find Jesus praying to the Father, as in John 17.

It is possible that the angel of the LORD was simply an angel with a special commission. There seem to be fewer difficulties in understanding the ministry of the angel of the LORD if we see the angel as a momentary revelation of God on this earth.

When we read in the Bible the many references to the angel of the LORD, we ask, "Was it an angel? Or was it God?" There are times today when we are aware of divine intervention in our lives that we ask the same question.

Chapter
8

The Warrior Angels

Joyce Story is a frail woman, weighing only eighty-five pounds. She is a scant five-foot-one. Severely handicapped with rheumatoid arthritis, she walks with a noticeable limp.

She was the treasurer of her Sunday school class, and every Tuesday morning it was her routine to go to the Security Pacific Bank on the corner of Van Buren and Arlington in Riverside, California, to deposit the offering from the class. It was already hot at ten o'clock one day in June 1985 as she went with her niece to the bank. The deposit was quickly made.

As Joyce and her niece left the bank they heard a woman scream, "Please don't! No! No! Help, help!"

There in the bank parking lot was a huge man, well over six feet tall, weighing about 250 pounds, wearing a ski mask. He was beating the shouting woman as he tried to steal her money bag. She had the handle of the bag wrapped around her arm, and the more the mugger pulled, the tighter it became. Then with a mighty blow he knocked the woman to the ground.

As tiny Joyce saw this something welled up deep within her spirit. There were many emotions, but the one she remembers feeling the most was grief—not just grief for the victim but grief for the assailant. Grief that one person would treat another so brutally.

In a moment the grief was replaced by an urgent feeling that God would have her take action. A small, handicapped woman confronting a large and violent criminal? Obediently, she limped toward the mugger. Raising a gnarled index finger and pointing at him, Joyce said softly, "No! In the name of Jesus, no!"

Joyce's niece, La Shell, watched fearfully at the strange encounter. Intent on stealing the money bag, the man continued to beat his victim while she was on the ground. Joyce kept limping slowly toward him, repeating calmly, "No! In the name of Jesus, no!" As she advanced, the handicapped woman became aware of a strong presence with her. Knowing she wasn't alone, all fear left her.

The man in the ski mask paused in his assault of the woman on the ground. He looked contemptuously at little Joyce, but then he looked up, over her head. He became startled; his eyes filled with terror. He began to back up as if in shock, saying, "Oh, oh, oh!" Then he turned and ran for his life.

What did he see? Joyce has no doubt. She knows she would not frighten anyone, but she was aware of an angel behind her. From the way the mugger looked, the warrior angel must have been at least nine feet tall.

Joyce helped the woman get up from the pavement and into the bank for first aid. The police were called and responded quickly. The officer making the report was skeptical about the angel. He did recognize the description of the mugger, however. The man had assaulted several people at different banks in the area, and the police said that he was not afraid of anyone—certainly not of a handicapped little woman. Joyce says, "There is no human explanation why this mugger was frightened of me. He could have snapped me like a pretzel. Praise the Lord, he was frightened of my angel."

The story came to us from Joyce Story's point of view. How interesting it would be if we were able to find the criminal with the ski mask and hear his account of the

THE WARRIOR ANGELS 77

angel that struck fear in his heart. Was it enough to make him "scared straight"? Was his life changed by this awesome encounter? In this case we do not know.

Mighty Warriors Dressed for Battle

There have been times when lives were changed by an encounter with warrior angels. The best-documented case of this happening occurred in the life of John Patton.

John Patton and his wife were pioneer missionaries to the New Hebrides Islands. Faithfully they tried to live out the Christian gospel and model a Christian lifestyle. They were met with hostility. They returned insults with kindness, hatred with love.

It soon became apparent that even their lives were in danger. There were threats that their home would be burned and the missionary couple murdered, but the Pattons felt called by God. Praying for divine protection, they continued to minister in a spirit of love.

Then one night they heard noises outside their small missionary compound. Looking out, they saw they were completely surrounded by the chief and his men with torches and spears. They were being true to their word. They had come to burn their home and kill the missionaries. The Pattons had no weapons. There was no earthly means of protection, but they could pray, and pray they did! Throughout the terror-filled night they prayed for God to send his angels to protect them. They prayed that this warlike tribe would someday find peace with God.

When the morning came, the tribe silently left. The Pattons were elated but very surprised. There seemed to be no reason for the war party to leave.

Others of fainter heart would have sailed away from the island looking for more hospitable mission territory, but the Pattons felt called by God to stay. Fearlessly yet gently and lovingly, they continued to witness but without any noticeable results.

A full year later the chief became a Christian. Finally John Patton was able to ask the question that had puzzled him for so long: "Chief, remember that night you came and surrounded our house? Your men all had spears and torches. What had you planned to do?"

The chief replied, "We came to kill you and burn everything you have."

"What kept you from doing it?" the missionary asked.

"We were afraid of all those men who were guarding your house," the chief replied.

"But there were no men," Patton replied. "We were alone, my wife and I."

"No, no," the chief insisted. "There were many men around your house. Big men. Giants. They were awesome. They had no torches but they glowed with a strange light, and each had a drawn sword in his hand. Who were they?"

Instinctively the missionary *knew*. He and his wife had prayed for protection, and God had sent his angels. The missionary also recognized that this was a teachable moment for the new convert. "Let me explain what you saw," Patton said as he opened his Bible to Second Kings, chapter 6. He read the biblical account of the time that the king of Aram sent his army to capture the prophet Elisha. During the night the army surrounded the place where Elisha was. In the morning, Elisha's helper saw that they were surrounded by an army with horses and chariots.

"What shall we do?" the man asked in fear.

" 'Don't be afraid,' the prophet answered. 'Those who are with us are more than those who are with them.' And Elisha prayed, 'O LORD, open his eyes so he may see.' Then the LORD opened the servant's eyes, and he looked and saw the hills full of horses and chariots of fire all around Elisha" (2 Kings 6:16–17).

Nightly Camping in Haiti—Kay Kallander

The voodoo drums began softly. Each hour their incessant throbbing became louder and more insistent. There was an almost hypnotic power in the compelling beat.

Kay had come as a missionary nurse, working in a clinic outside of Port-au-Prince, Haiti. She shared a small house with another woman missionary. A low fence surrounded their home, marking the property boundaries. It certainly was not high enough to be a deterrent to anyone who might want to break into the house.

Every night the drums would serve notice that the voodoo rituals were taking place. In the morning as Kay made her way to the clinic, she would see evidence of the nightly ceremonies: blood, fragments of animal parts, and cult objects. It was unpleasant at best; at times it was gruesome.

There was trouble every night. Kay tried not to think of it when she went to bed at the end of a long day. As the drums began, she would pray for those caught in the spell of voodoo. And she would pray for her own safety.

During the day at the clinic Kay often treated wounds and injuries that resulted from the hysteria of the nightly rituals. Before dark she would return to her home. It was a scary place to be, but Kay had told God she would go where he wanted her to go—and she was convinced God wanted her to use her nursing skills here where they were so needed.

Poverty was everywhere. In desperation the poor would break into houses and steal anything of value.

According to United States standards, the two women missionaries had only modest belongings, but in that area of Haiti what they had was worth stealing. And far worse things often happened to women living alone.

Yet the two missionaries had no problems, and their home was never broken into. Night after night the drums would beat, and Kay was aware that violence was taking place all around where they lived.

One day a middle-aged Haitian man suffering with pain came to the dental clinic. The dentist did oral surgery and extensive repair work on his mouth. Because of the amount of work, the man stayed quite a while. On this day Kay was working with pain management and had time to talk with the patient. Finding him to be friendly and open, she asked a question that had been troubling her. "Why is it that with all the problems in our neighborhood and the break-ins that happen nightly, there has never been any theft at our house? It would seem that we would be a natural target."

"No one would ever enter your yard," the Haitian replied. "Everyone knows about the guards you have."

"The guards?" Kay asked incredulously. "What guards?"

"The guards you have on duty every night. There are four of them. Big, big men. Dark, very dark men. One stands on each corner of your property. They are very frightening. No one would dare to come into your house. Everyone knows about them. Lady, nobody will cause you any trouble."

Who were these guards? The missionary had not hired any guards. Often they looked out of their windows at night. Never had they seen a guard—or any other person—on their property.

Kay is certain that they were angels of God, unseen to

the missionaries but clearly visible to potential trouble-makers.

"The angel of the LORD encamps around those who fear him, and he delivers them," Kay quotes from Psalm 34:7. "At our house in Haiti we had four angels who camped out every night."

These warrior angels are awesome! Ask a person what an angel looks like and chances are that he or she may describe a beautiful blonde woman with wings—sometimes angels do appear that way. Ask what a cherub looks like, and you will be told that it is a little childlike angel. But not in the Bible. The cherubim (the plural of cherub) in the Bible are warrior angels. They are the first to appear in the Bible, in Genesis 3:24, where they guard the Garden of Eden so that no one can enter. In Solomon's temple there were carved cherubim that were thirty feet high with wings that were each fifteen feet wide—a far cry from the cute cherubim found on greeting cards. Throughout the Bible the cherubim are not always described in the same way. Perhaps the form in which these spirit beings manifest themselves changes according to the function they serve.

We learn much about angels from the Bible and from experience. Some things about angels remain mysteries to us. We have noted that angels are not usually visible, but when it serves God's purposes they can be seen. It is interesting that there are times when some people who are present see angels and others do not. Our human logic would tell us that angels would be seen by those who were people of faith, while the angels remained unseen by those who did not believe. But as often is the case in spiritual matters, human logic does not always hold the answer. For example, Missionary Patton did not see angels, but the tribesmen coming to murder did.

One principle seems clear: Angels are seen by those

who have a need to see them. How is this done? Some things remain a mystery. There is a range of evidence found even in this book. Some who've experienced angelic encounters have been very aware of the presence of angels but have not seen them. Others have seen the angels. It's interesting that all appearances of angels are not alike. The descriptions that people give of angels vary from what appears to be an ordinary person to a moving sphere of light. And yes, some do see angels that look like our traditional image of the heavenly host.

How do we account for this difference of form that angels take when they materialize? Do angels simply choose in what form they will appear? Or do differing orders or ranks of angels manifest themselves each in their own way? The Bible nowhere answers this question. Professors of theology may speculate when they teach angelology, but your speculation is as good as theirs. We simply do not know.

Nick Stoia's Story

"The flat had seemed to be just right for our family. It was a two-story, yellow brick building with the upstairs identical to the downstairs on the west side of Detroit. When we moved in, we had the ground floor. My wife's cousin, who owned the building, lived with her family on the second floor.

"Later the flat above us was rented to a couple who seemed nice enough when they moved in. To our consternation, the man became increasingly irritable.

"We learned that he was suffering from Graves' disease, caused by overactivity of the thyroid. When his medication wasn't right, his eyes would bulge or seem to pop. He would become very nervous and irritable.

"One day he was very stressed out. He stood on our

front porch, threatening to come in and kill us. It was frightening. Seeing him with his face red, his eyes bulging—and watching his constant activity—made us realize he was far from normal. We knew that his threats were not to be taken lightly. He was dangerous in this condition.

"We stayed on our guard throughout the evening. Before going to bed, my wife, Sandy, and I prayed for God's protection over us. We prayed for God to set a hedge of angels around us to protect us. My wife fell asleep, while I stayed awake, continuing to pray for our safety.

"I became aware that we were not alone in the room. An angel was standing guard. He was tall, about six-foot-four, and with a very muscular build. His entire being was radiating a light, something I had not seen before. If I had to name a color, the closest I could come to it would be a very deep cobalt blue. The look on his face reminded me of the special Marine guards stationed around important places like the White House: extremely proud of the duty they are performing and not somebody you'd want to mess with.

"I was filled with a feeling of safety. God had sent his angel. I was allowed to see this angel so that I would know that my prayers were being answered and that God would keep us safe and protect us. Since the angel was standing guard, there was no reason for me to stay awake. Free of worry, I fell sound asleep.

"The next day we rented a truck and moved out.

"What's neat, as I think back about this experience, is that it illustrates how God cares about the day-to-day affairs of just common people. God doesn't send his angels just to the leaders, the king of Israel, or the head of a church. He cares for all his children—even me."

Chapter
9

The Angels of Encouragement

The Barefoot Angel

In the academic realm, Dr. V. Raymond Edman was highly regarded as a scholar. The author of nineteen books, he served with distinction for twenty-five years as president of Wheaton College in Wheaton, Illinois. He was our personal friend. He played a most important part in our lives, especially on June 16, 1952, on which day my husband-to-be and I both graduated from Wheaton College in the morning. In the evening we were married. It was "Prexy," Dr. Edman, who presided at both ceremonies.

In 1923 the Edmans themselves had been married in Quito, Ecuador, and then began missionary service in the Andean highlands in western South America. It was pioneer mission work, and they chose to live on the outskirts of a city so that they would have contact both with the Spanish-speaking citizens on the streets and in the marketplaces and with the thousands of Quichua-speaking Indians who passed their doorway on the way to market.

The assignment was a difficult one. The Indians who passed by were shy and suspicious. They were intimidated by the people living in the city.

"The people were quite unfriendly," Edman wrote, "and some were fanatical in their bitter opposition to our presence in their city. On occasion small crowds would gather to hurl insults, punctuated by stones both large and small. Now and then, children would parade in the dusty street before our home and repeat what they had been taught to say against us. The Indians from the countryside were especially timid about having any friendly contact with us because of intimidation by some of the townspeople. As a result, it was often difficult to get the bare necessities of life—fruits and vegetables, or charcoal for the kitchen stove."

Added to these physical factors was an inward sense of human loneliness. The missionary couple kept close to God but felt isolated from people. This was especially discouraging for them because they had a great desire to share their faith with the very folk who insisted on shutting them out.

They had rented a rather typical house. Across the front of the lot was the usual high iron fence with a large gate of grillwork. Whenever they were not in the front part of the house, the Edmans kept the gate locked with an iron chain and a great padlock. There was constant danger that someone would slip into the house and steal whatever was of value.

One day the missionary couple were eating their noon meal in the small open patio behind their house. They heard a rattling on the gate as though someone were asking for admission. Edman went to see who might be there. He saw what appeared to be an Indian woman. She was knocking on the chain with the padlock. She did not have a bundle on her shoulder, like the women who sold vegetables. She wore the large heavy hat of the mountain women, a typical blue shawl over her shoulders, a white homespun waist with its primitive embroidery, a dress of coarse woolen cloth, and had the customary beads on her wrists. She was barefoot. Curious, the young missionary went to see what she might want.

The woman began to speak softly, in the mixture of Spanish and Quichua that was typical of the Indians who lived fairly close to town. "Are you the people who have come to tell us about the living God?" she inquired.

Edman was startled. No one had ever asked that before. Somewhat surprised he answered, "Mamita (*little mother*, the customary term for a woman of her years), yes, we are."

The woman raised her hand that was still inside the locked gate and began to pray, asking for God's blessing on the Edmans, that they would have the courage to carry out the service committed to them, that they would find joy in doing God's bidding, and that many would hear and obey the words of the Gospel.

She smiled at the startled missionary. Her eyes fairly shone as she said, "Dios le bendiga" (God bless you), bowed, and left.

Edman was astonished. Quickly he remembered it was the heat of the day and that she should come in and eat with them. In a matter of seconds he had unlocked the gate and stepped out to call her back. She did not have time to go more than five or ten yards.

But she was not there! Not a soul was in sight. It was siesta time and the street was deserted. He could see nearly a half mile in either direction. Edman had been on the track team in school, and at the age of twenty-four he was still in good shape. He sprinted to the closest gate, nearly a block away. Hastily he inquired of the two men there, "Did an Indian woman just come in here?"

"No, sir," they replied. "We have been right here in the gate for an hour or more, and there has been no one on this street."

Edman returned home, locked the gate, and joined his wife at the dinner table. "Where have you been so long?" she asked. Her husband repeated his strange encounter.

Later he wrote, "For days afterward my own heart remained strangely moved. It burned within me as I remembered that Indian woman's prayer, and it was strengthened by the blessing she had pronounced upon me. There seemed to be an aroma indescribably sweet and indefinable that certainly did not come from the flowers in the garden.

"After some days, I began to reflect upon the word in Hebrews 13:2: 'Be not forgetful to entertain strangers: for thereby some have entertained angels unawares' (KJV). I began to understand that the Almighty had none of his earthly servants at hand to encourage two young missionaries, so he was pleased to send an angel from heaven."

The Angel Touch

Jeanette Gable was very apprehensive about her surgery. On the day of her surgery she could hardly talk. When they took her into the holding room to wait for her turn in the operating room, her fears grew. The wait seemed so long. A nurse noticed her shaking. "Oh! You must be cold," the nurse said and brought some blankets to cover her.

Jeanette was thankful for the thoughtfulness of the nurse. The warmth of the blankets helped, but her shaking continued. It wasn't the cold that caused the shaking. It was fear, a fear of the surgery. The wait had been long; the room was empty now. Everyone else had been taken into surgery except for one woman at Jeanette's left.

Jeanette had talked with her surgeon about her fears. She wondered why they had not given her any sedation to help her through this long, lonely wait. The shaking was violent now. Jeanette cried out in prayer, "Lord, I can accept any thing you have in store for me. Just please give me peace and calmness."

Over and over she repeated her plea for peace. She had never prayed so desperately in her life.

Jeanette felt a hand pressing into the hollow between her front shoulder and collar bone. It was a firm, reassuring touch, but no one was there! She lifted her head and looked around. The holding room was empty except for the other patient, some distance away, with her face toward the wall. There was no human who could have touched her.

It was then that Jeanette realized that her prayer had been answered. She had stopped shaking. A wonderful, warm, reassuring peace filled her from her toes to the top of her head. She was completely relaxed.

Soon the surgeon came and told her that they would be ready for her in surgery shortly. Then the anesthesiologist came, skillfully attached an IV into her arm, and told the nurse to put a relaxant into the IV. Jeanette smiled and watched the procedure. She was relaxed already. The doctor later told her she was already asleep when they took her into the operating room.

The surgery was a success. Immediately Jeanette gave credit to a good doctor and to answered prayers.

"I did not share this with anyone for about six months," Jeanette told us, "because so many are skeptical about angels. Never had I experienced such calmness and stillness in my life. I am most thankful for this experience. I know God sent his angel (my guardian angel) to hover over me and give me peace."

Kathleen Kenyon—the Unexpected Angels

Kathleen Kenyon is a registered nurse who practices in suburban Chicago. Four years ago she became one of a team of nurses who attended young Michelle Stevens around the clock.

Michelle had almost drowned in a drainpipe near her home when she was seventeen months old. When Kathleen started working this new assignment, she was told that Michelle, now almost five years old, was a "vegetable." She had been severely retarded by the anoxia of the drowning. She couldn't speak because she had a tracheostomy and was fed through a gastronomy tube.

As Kathleen cared for Michelle, she wondered if anything could be done to break through to her, to tap the intelligence that she sometimes thought she saw behind the little girl's eyes.

Then one day, the nurse on the shift before hers said, "A strange thing happened. I was chatting to Michelle as I usually do, and getting no response. But when I mentioned my collection of angels, she seemed suddenly interested and alert."

Kathleen filed the information away and went in to change Michelle and pray her to sleep as usual.

But the next night Michelle wasn't sleepy, so Kathleen began to talk to her. Remembering what the other nurse had said, Kathleen commented, "I hear you're interested in angels."

The change in Michelle was immediate and pronounced. Her features became animated and she blinked the universal signal for "Yes." And she continued, "Yes! Yes! Yes!"

Kathleen wondered if the other nurse had showed her some angel figurines. "Are angels little?" she asked, attempting conversation.

Michelle blinked—a definitive "No!"

Surprised but pleased, Kathleen said, "Are they big?" "Yes."

"As tall as this room?"

Again, "Yes."

"Are they in white?"—"Yes."
"Do they look like women?"—"No."
"Do they look like men?"—"Yes."

As the conversation continued, Kathleen able to ask only yes-no questions, it began to dawn on her that Michelle not only comprehended her completely but was describing in detail something she had seen. And slowly she realized that this lonely, locked-in girl who was assumed to be a vegetable had been comforted and befriended—by angels.

That conversation was an opening in more ways than one. It turned out that Michelle was far from being a vegetable—she was depressed by the abrupt departure of a nurse for whom she had come to care very deeply. Describing her angelic visitors was the opening of a door not only between her and Kathleen but also between Michelle and others.

Today, nearly four years later, Michelle and Kathleen are prayer partners. Michelle can't wait to get a specially outfitted computer because she wants to write books.

Kathleen Kenyon can't wait, either. "I'm dying to read everything Michelle has to say!" she says.

Laura Benét—Not Alone

Our daughter, Sharon Linnea Scott, lives in New York City with her husband, Bob. One of Sharon's favorite stories of God's care happened back in 1976, when she was a college student new to the city.

"When I left the safety of friends and family in the midwest to move to New York City, I had no idea that I would meet one of my best friends on the street—or that she would be seventy-three years older than I!

"She came into my life one autumn day in 1976 on a No. 3 bus that rumbled down New York's Fifth Avenue.

As the bus stopped at 12th Street, an elderly passenger was having trouble negotiating the last long step to the ground. A voice right behind me barked, 'Young man, this is a kneeling bus. Would you be kind enough to let it kneel?'

"The driver, put out, lowered the bus step. I had to smile. The sturdy voice belonged to a woman who herself would not see eighty again.

"I ran into her again when we were both shopping in a local deli, then a few days later on the street as she struggled with a large package. I offered to help. As we walked, I discovered that her name was Laura and that her apartment was only two blocks from my college dormitory in Greenwich Village. Over the next weeks and months we kept running into each other, and a friendship began to form. We eventually met for dinner at a local restaurant called Shakespeare's. She seemed interested in my plans to be a writer; I felt I'd done a lonely old lady a good turn.

"Then one winter day Laura invited me up to her homey, one-room apartment. The walls were lined top-to-bottom with books (from which old newspaper clippings were forever escaping) and boxes of letters.

"She'd brought up her mail, and she handed me a poetry magazine. 'I can't quite read it,' she said. 'Have I anything in this one?'

"Laura—a poet? I looked at the brown cover, and sure enough, there was her name. 'Why yes, you do,' I said. 'I Let the Trees Know I Was There.'

"A satisfied smile crossed her face as she sat at her small writing desk in the afternoon light—and recited the entire poem from memory.

"My amazement had just begun. As I took the magazine to the shelf, I saw a copy of *King David* by the American writer Stephen Vincent Benét. The gold-embossed volume, inscribed by Benét to his parents, was the first to roll off the presses back in 1923.

"When I asked her where she got it, she answered simply, 'Why, Tibbie was my baby brother.' Laura was Stephen Vincent Benét's older sister. She'd just turned ninety-two.

"Sensing my astonishment, Laura looked at me with eyes that danced merrily. 'My dear,' she said, 'you must always give people room to surprise you. If you don't, they'll probably act like the boring people you expect them to be. You must give God room to surprise you, too!'

"As our friendship deepened, Laura surprised me again and again. How much those eyes, now glossy with cataracts, had seen! She wove wonderful stories of people and places in a time I never knew. I learned more about the literary world from this older woman with her soft, braided hair and 'proper' hats than from any of my college professors.

"Sixty years ago, the Benéts were one of America's foremost literary families. Laura herself had more than twenty books to her name: biographies, children's books, poems. She'd also trained as a social worker at the turn of the century, putting in selfless years at Manhattan's Spring Street Settlement.

" 'God takes care of us,' she'd tell me, 'and he expects us to take care of one another.' Laura's faith was important to her, and she never missed a Sunday at church.

"Despite the difference in our ages, she insisted on calling me 'Little Sister.' As the months, then years passed, and our friendship deepened, I also became more worried about Laura's living by herself. More than once I prayed that she wouldn't be left alone in time of crisis.

"Then one summer Sunday morning our churches

were meeting together, but Laura wasn't there. After the service I rushed to her building. One look at the building manager's face and I knew that my fears were well-founded.

"Laura had had a heart attack alone in her room the night before. She'd fallen and broken her hip. Unable to crawl to the phone, she'd lain on the floor all night long. 'We found her this morning,' the manager said. 'She's in the hospital now.'

"I ran to St. Vincent's Hospital. A heart attack! She'd been alone, in pain all night—and after I'd specifically prayed so hard that this wouldn't happen! When the nurse at the admitting desk said, 'Are you family?' I said yes without thinking twice.

"In the cardiac unit's intensive care wing, I took Laura's hand and said, 'Laura, I love you. I'm sorry, so sorry that you were alone.'

"Laura looked at me and shook her head. 'But I wasn't alone, Little Sister. There was a man with me, a young man. It was so dark, I couldn't even see if he was black or white. He said, "Laura, when I'm in trouble or afraid, I pray to the Lord." So he held my hand, and we prayed and sang hymns together all night.'

"I almost said, 'But there couldn't have been a man. The manager said your door was locked from the inside.' But then I remembered praying that Laura wouldn't be alone in time of crisis. And she hadn't been. Instead of being isolated and frightened, she had been consoled and comforted all through that difficult night. I knew that God in his mercy had answered my prayer and sent an angel to stay with her.

"Laura herself had always assured me that 'God takes care of us.' And she also counseled, 'You must give God room to surprise you.' Thanks to Laura, I know for certain that both are absolutely true." (Adapted from

Guideposts magazine. Copyright ® 1990 by Guideposts Associates, Inc., Carmel, NY 10510.)

Angel of the Commonplace

There are times when angels appear at a dramatic moment in a life-or-death situation, or a time of great importance. But not always. There are many times when angels have come quietly and left people wondering why.

Mr. Pace saw an angel, a tiny, white, brilliant angel, glowing as the gown blew in the gentle breeze. It left him breathless and wondering. Why had the angel come to him? It was not a guardian angel saving him from harm. It did not speak. It gave no specific message. Yet it was real. It left a deep impression on him.

Later he began to pray, "God, show me why, the purpose of my seeing an angel."

Months later, he relates, "It hit my spirit with a big whammy: It is God's love surrounding you."

A great revelation? No, not really. That message has been the basis for Sunday school lessons for preschoolers through adults for years. But for Mr. Pace it was a doctrine that had suddenly come alive. After the brief moment with the angel he not only knew about God's love but he also felt this love surrounding him. "It was a beautiful serendipity," he tells everyone.

Fear of Flying

At times an angel comes for what seems to be simply personal reasons. Elsie Valleau's problem was a fear of flying. Hardly a major concern in the big scheme of things, it was a real problem for Elsie. The day came when she had no alternative. She had to fly. She packed the night before so that she would be able to get an early start to the airport. Elsie's stress level was so high that she had trouble falling asleep.

About two in the morning, Elsie felt a presence in the room, as if someone was watching her. At the foot of the bed she saw an angel dressed in a most beautiful lace-eyelet gown. The angel paused for only a moment, then it floated across the room and went right through the closed door.

In the morning Elsie was ready to fly. She had no fear. Although the angel had not said a word, its presence had left her with a sense of peace. And love—a new love for God.

It only was a moment, but the results of that moment have lasted the rest of Elsie's life. Fear of flying has been replaced with a love for travel.

Dial 911 for an Angel

In November 1989, Jim Wilson was new at his job as a police officer, working at the Greater Pittsburgh Airport. He was working a second eight-hour shift. As he walked down a deserted hallway, he saw an older man stop and slump over against the wall. Jim ran quickly; the man collapsed, and Jim helped him to the floor. The police-man checked and found no pulse. The man had stopped breathing.

Jim called the paramedics on his radio. It was his first emergency, and he was all alone. The responsibility seemed awesome, the classroom training so remote. He knew that it was up to him to take action until the paramedics arrived, but could he? "I had been trained on what to do," Jim says, "but I found I wasn't thinking clearly. Just then I heard a woman behind me say, 'I'm a nurse. I'll do the chest compression if you do the rescue breathing.'"

Jim began the mouth-to-mouth breathing while the woman did compressions. They worked together until the paramedics arrived and took over. The man revived.

"The strangest thing happened," Jim said. "I stood up and looked for the nurse to thank her, but there was no one there. She had suddenly appeared from nowhere when I needed help; once the crisis was over, she simply vanished."

Jim Wilson believes that angels know CPR, and he is convinced that one did compressions in the Pittsburgh Airport when there was no one else to help. Now he makes his rounds with a new confidence born of the assurance that with God's help he will be able to do what is right and necessary in any situation. God's angel came at a time he needed encouragement, and the memory of that event will always strengthen him.

Angels Praying

Florence Cales shared the concern of her family. She and her husband were living with her son, Seymour, and his family in Whittier, California. The past two weeks had been difficult for everyone.

First there was the night Seymour didn't come home from work. After waiting anxiously, his wife, Mary Ethel, had called his work, but everyone had gone home, and there was no answer. It was not like Seymour to be late coming home, much less be gone overnight without telling his family.

In the morning, Seymour called from the hospital. He had become sick at work; an ambulance had been called, and he was taken to the hospital. That night he had an emergency appendectomy. In the rush no one had thought to notify his family.

Seymour had been home for a week when his family

saw that he suddenly had a violent attack. They called the ambulance and rushed him to Studebaker Hospital in Norwalk. His family doctor, Dr. Kim, immediately called in a heart specialist, Dr. Middo.

The doctors told the family they were doing all they could, but Seymour was in serious condition. He had suffered both a stroke and a heart attack, and his right side was paralyzed. The doctors sent the family home but told them to expect a call from the hospital.

Mary Ethel, Seymour's wife, knew that she needed sleep but was too nervous to rest. She stayed in the living room, praying.

Florence, Seymour's mother, was concerned both for her son in the hospital and her husband. She decided that the best thing she could do would be to go to bed with her husband and hope that he could get some sleep. She stayed awake, greatly disturbed in spirit but praying silently for her grown son.

Suddenly Florence was aware of an angel at the foot of the bed. The figure was all light, shining brightly. Florence raised up to see the angel more closely when the angel spoke. "Don't worry," the angel said, reassuringly. "You go to sleep. Let me pray."

Immediately Florence was filled with a sense of peace. All worries were gone. She knew that Seymour would recover. She fell asleep and slept soundly until morning.

The doctors were truly surprised. Seymour did recover and lived thirteen more years. His mother was not surprised. After all, she knew that the angels had been praying.

Chapter
10

The Strengthening Angels

Perhaps the ministry of angels that is best-known is that of guardian angels, but angels don't always save us from physical harm. In biblical times, as in life today, we find that angels sometimes intervene by giving strength for the challenge or ordeal that may lie ahead.

Some people find this role harder to understand; often strengthening angels aren't even mentioned in theological discussions of angelology, but those who have experienced this kind of intervention find it a powerful experience.

Let's start by looking at one of our favorite present-day encounters, which happened in our hometown of Riverside, California.

Estela Vera's Story

"The infection came two years ago. As a registered nurse I took all precautions and followed the doctor's orders. In time the infection was gone, but there was a lasting side effect: I was deaf.

"Perhaps the hardest thing about losing my hearing was that it meant the end of my career as well. If I could not hear my patients, I could no longer give them the care they needed. I was far too young to retire, and although I could no longer hear, the rest of my body was strong and well. Surely there were other ways I could support myself that would bring fulfillment and satisfaction.

"I have always loved to sew. Why not become a professional seamstress? I asked myself. I enrolled in a leading fashion and design school. My loss of hearing was a disadvantage, but I could read and use my mind, my eyes, and my hands. I became one of the top students and won several awards for designs. My specialty was going to be wedding dresses. In three months I would graduate. Anticipation grew daily as I looked forward to an exciting new career.

"The loss of my hearing, the loss of my profession as a nurse, were difficult adjustments for me to make. I never could have coped with my loss without God's help. Little did I know that an even bigger adjustment was ahead of me.

"What a surprise! My daughter, her husband, and my grandchildren drove from Salinas to be with me on Easter. It was one o'clock Saturday morning when they arrived. We would celebrate the resurrection of our Lord as a family. But since they were unexpected, I had no milk or juice for the little ones, and I wanted to buy eggs that we could decorate together for Easter.

"The next day my son, Mingo, drove my old Cadillac, taking my daughter, Martha, and me to the store. When we came to the corner of Bonner and Polk Streets, I saw that the driver of an ice-cream truck was in trouble. A man had a stranglehold around his neck and was holding a knife against his throat. 'Mingo,' I shouted, 'drive close to the truck so that criminal will know we see him. Surely he'll stop if he knows someone is watching.'

"Mingo began to tailgate the truck, blowing the horn, but I was wrong. Nothing seemed to faze the attacker. 'Stop at the Seven-Eleven Store,' I shouted. 'We'll dial 911 and call the police.'

"Mingo turned the car into the store's parking lot, dashed to the telephone, dialed 911, and gave the police the report of the crime in progress, describing the truck and giving its location.

"I thought that would be the end of the adventure . . . but how wrong I was. As we were driving home on Hole Avenue, we saw the ice-cream truck stopped at the intersection of Cynthia Street. On the side of the street a struggle was going on. The ice-cream truck driver and another man were trying to hold the attacker down. Mingo slammed on his brakes and dashed out to help subdue the assailant. Martha rushed across the street to dial 911 and give the police an update on the location of the crime. I got out of the car, frustrated at the thought that there was nothing I could do.

"Suddenly the thief broke loose and dashed to the ice-cream truck in a desperate effort to get away. As he gunned the motor, I had a terrifying realization—he was purposely driving the truck directly at me. I'll never forget the look in his eyes. I saw raw, naked evil. He was trying to kill me, to crush me against my car. He was doing it deliberately.

" 'O God,' I cried, 'I don't want to die. Send your angels to save my life.' And I began to quote Psalm 34:7, 'The angel of the Lord encamps around them who fear him, and delivers them.'

"It was then I saw the angel. He was tall, very tall. He was surrounded by bright light. His clothes were luminous, a kind of glowing pink. He had a kind expression on his face, and beautiful, compassionate eyes. His hands were stretched out in love. Instantly I knew that my life would be saved. I was at peace. The angel gathered me in his arms and held me.

"They tell me that the paramedics gave me CPR for five minutes. One of my legs was completely severed. A spoke from the hubcap of my car had passed clear through my body. My body was crushed. I lost several pints of blood. The doctors were amazed that I survived. 'It was a miracle,' one said. I knew that he was right. God had spared my life. He had sent his angel to give me peace at the time of the accident. That peace stayed with me through the several operations that followed and the difficult times of physical therapy.

"Although my leg is gone, I have so much to be thankful for. I am still alive. God answered my prayer, a grandmother's prayer, that I might be able to help my family, especially my grandchildren, come to know the faith in the Lord that means everything to me.

"I still have the use of my hands. I still have one leg, the leg I need to run my sewing machine. But making elegant wedding dresses is no longer so important to me. Instead, my burden is to sew blankets for the homeless. My dream now is to have my friends give me the remnants of their material so that I can sew dresses for children who have no new clothes. I want to gather dolls that girls no longer want. I want to sew new clothes and dress the dolls so that I can give them to little girls who have never had a doll of their own.

"And I want to talk to Sam, the man who did this to me. My heart breaks for him. They told me that he was all alone in the courtroom. He had no family or friends who cared enough to be there for him. I learned that he was a troubled child, that he was a delinquent teen, and now as an adult he was on parole from prison when he ran me down.

"I want Sam to know that God cares for him, that I care, too, and that I'm praying for him."

* * *

It's understandable that some are puzzled by Estela's story. If the angel was present when Estela was about to be hit by the ice-cream truck, why didn't the angel protect her and keep her from harm? Isn't that what guardian angels are supposed to do? The Bible—and this book—give many accounts of guardian angels who have kept people from injury, often in miraculous ways. If we had our way, angels would always protect us. We would never fall, never have an accident, never be injured. Most likely, angels do protect us more often than we realize. God, in his wisdom, knows that it is not always best to keep everyone everywhere from all accidents and injuries.

But angels are not always guardian angels. In the Scripture and in life today we find angels who sometimes minister by giving strength for the challenge or ordeal that may lie ahead. Many people have never thought of angels who strengthen. Even books about angels rarely mention strengthening angels, and the standard books on theology do not list this angelic function in their discussions of angelology.

To understand this important ministry, let us first consider Estela's experience and then compare it with the biblical evidence.

When the Fox Television Network decided to do a program on angels, they called and asked us for a person who had an experience with an angel. After meeting Estela, they decided to film her story. The segment was videotaped in our home with angels from Marilynn's collection in the background. The interviewer and the camera crew had no doubts that Estela was certain that she had seen an angel. The experience was so profound that Estela knows it was real.

The angel came before Estela was hit by the ice-cream truck. She was not in pain and was in full control of her senses. Estela says without hesitation, "It really happened. I saw the angel come to me."

This came at a time of special need. Estela had been

through a great amount of suffering with the loss of her hearing and the loss of her profession. She was about to go through great pain, several operations, the loss of a leg, and a long period of recuperation. The experience with the angel gave Estela strength to endure all that was to follow in the months ahead. Instead of asking, "Why did this happen to me?" Estela would always talk about how thankful she was to God for giving her the strength and the will to face her ordeal. "God was so good to send his angel to me," she told us. "That experience has given me great comfort and peace. I know God will be with me and help me through whatever may be needed."

The appearance of the angel gave Estela a clear vision of her purpose in life. From her hospital bed she explained that her life had been spared and that the angel came to her to help her put God in the center of her life, using her to help her family all come to a personal faith in Christ, and to use her talents, especially her sewing, to help the poor.

What impressed us most was Estela's complete lack of bitterness. She harbored no anger at the man who had caused her such pain. Instead of hatred, we found forgiveness and compassion. Her heart was breaking for the man who had tried to kill her. Instead of hatred, Estela has peace and joy. "The peace comes from God," Estela explains. "The coming of the angel at the time of my need touched my life so that I will never be the same."

Estela's angel did not speak. This is true of many of the angel experiences that people have shared with us. Merely being aware of the angel's presence is often all that is needed for a person to have what he or she regards as a forcible, convincing encounter with the Almighty God. It lifts all of life above the routine and often gives a divine perspective so that a person faces life with a new perspective.

In Genesis 32 we read the story of Jacob's wrestling with an angel. This is not a guardian angel who protects Jacob. In fact, the angel touches Jacob's hip, so his hip was wrenched, and Jacob left Peniel with a limp. But after this encounter Jacob was a changed man. Instead of being a cheat and a scoundrel, he became a prince with God. Before the encounter Jacob feared for his life and the life of his family. After this encounter he moves with faith and confidence, seeing life from a divine perspective.

The supreme example of the strengthening ministry of angels is found in the life of Christ. Jesus goes to the Garden of Gethsemane, where he agonizes in prayer. Jesus knew that before him was the anguish and suffering of the Cross. Every Christian knows how he prayed: "Father, if you are willing, take this cup from me; yet not my will, but yours be done." Few Christians remember the next verse (Luke 22:43): "An angel from heaven appeared to him and strengthened him."

In the hour of his greatest need the heavenly Father sent an angel to Jesus to strengthen him! The angel could have protected Jesus from harm. Jesus himself said that he could call twelve legions of angels (Matthew 26:53)— far more guardian angels than would be necessary to protect him. Rather, he chose to do his Father's will. The angel did not keep him from being betrayed, humiliated, scourged, and crucified. The angel did strengthen him so that he could face the Cross, endure all the suffering, and be victorious.

Kathy Hill—Climbing the Angel Ladder

It was July 1986. F.C. was shocked to learn that he had tumors on the brain. Not just one but five—and three of the tumors were the size of golf balls. All were malignant. His doctor sent him for surgery to the M. D. Anderson Cancer Center in Houston.

F.C. knew the seriousness of the situation. The surgeon had explained that they might not be able to remove all the tumors—that the surgery itself was a high risk with no guarantee that F.C. would survive. If he did, no one could predict what quality of life he might have.

For F.C. there was no choice. The tumors were causing such pain and fierce headaches that to do nothing would be out of the question. He was still in his forties. As long as there was a chance, he would go for it.

Sleep did not come easily in the night before the surgery. F.C. was awake, worrying. He was not a religious man. F.C.'s family were committed Christians, but F.C. himself had no faith to comfort him. For a long while he lay awake in the dark hospital room.

All at once a light appeared in the right corner of his room. The wall and ceiling seemed to open up and were replaced by the most incredibly beautiful light. As F.C. watched, astonished, the brightness seemed to open, and he saw a great staircase. An angel in a white robe loosely belted at the waist, was standing on the stairs. F.C. strained to get a glimpse of the man's face, but the light was so intensely bright and vibrant in the area of the angel's face that F.C. could not make out any features.

The angel did not speak. Nor did F.C. There seemed no need for words; communication was happening at a much deeper level than speech. The heavenly presence was like a benediction. F.C. felt at peace. He did not pray with words, but his heart was filled with the presence of God.

Early the next morning F.C. shared his strange encounter with his family. They had been praying for their father, but the last thing they had expected to hear F.C. talk about was an angel. They took it as a sign that F.C. would be healed.

In the operating room the surgeons began their work, but their patient began to hemorrhage so severely they had to stop their planned operation and work to stop the bleeding. They had been unsuccessful in their attempt to remove the five tumors.

A blood clot formed and caused F.C. to lose his speech. Totally paralyzed on the right side, two weeks after the surgery F.C. was sent home to die.

The experience had been shattering to the family. "Daddy saw the angel," his daughter, Kathy Hill, kept repeating. "There had to be a reason for that angel. It must mean that Daddy will recover. We can't give up on him now."

Her mother and sisters agreed. No matter what the doctors said, the family refused to give up on him. They invented their own type of physical therapy and worked on his paralyzed arm and leg several times a day. They patiently fed him. They encouraged him to try to talk. At first there were sounds, then with great effort F.C. was able to speak, at first only a word or two at a time that could be understood.

Four months later, on Thanksgiving Day, F.C. walked again. His physical condition improved rapidly. In time he was able to speak as well as ever.

In December, F.C. went for the first visit with his doctors since the surgery. The doctors were amazed to find no evidence of any tumors. F.C. and his family were not surprised. The healing, they knew, had come from God. The presence of the angel had been a sign that F.C. would recover.

F.C. reestablished his construction business. He was

busy in the work he knew well, and it seemed that his problems were behind him.

But only six months later F.C. became sick with stomach cancer, which new illness he and his family faced with optimism. But a year and a half later, F.C. died.

"I was confused," his daughter Kathy said. "I could not understand how this could happen. Daddy had seen the angel, and I thought that meant that everything would be all right—that he would live and be healthy to a ripe old age. After all, he was only fifty.

"But looking back, I see what it all meant. Daddy was never a religious man. Of course he believed in God, but he had only been inside a church once. Daddy was a good man, but he had never been saved by the blood of Jesus.

"After he recovered from the brain tumors, he became a Christian and began to go to church. He was a changed man—more loving—and taking time to spend with his children and grandchildren.

"I believe that the angel changed him in ways that no one else ever could. Although he is no longer with us, I believe that Daddy was carried to heaven in the arms of that angel. That is such a tremendous comfort to all of his family. We know he was given everlasting life— something he would never have received without his illness and the appearance of the beautiful angel in his room that night."

Chapter
11

Messenger Angels

In the eternal scheme of things, angels have delivered some pretty important messages that have changed the course of history. For example, on the first Christmas Day they gave the news that "Today in the town of David a Savior has been born to you." They have sometimes been the bearers of important information in the lives of ordinary human beings.

Vicky was eighteen, pregnant, poor, and scared. She didn't know what to do. She watched a sonogram of her baby and knew that an abortion was out of the question. After many nights of crying herself to sleep, an angel appeared to her in a dream. The angel, dressed in blue, had unusual beauty. "Everything will be fine," the angel assured Vicky. "Don't be afraid. You and your baby will be taken care of."

The angel held Vicky comfortingly in her arms. Then she gave her a glimpse of the future. Vicky saw her baby, healthy and beautiful. A loving couple came, and the angel gently placed the baby in their arms. Next, Vicki saw the baby as a grown woman, mature and happy. She had the assurance that God would work all this for good for her child. Then the angel placed a light that was like a growing warmth that stayed in Vicky's heart.

Vicky woke feeling warm and wonderful. That day she met a woman who told her of a support group for unmarried girls. Within twenty-four hours she was attending this support group, finding not only healing for her emotions but also the information on choices she could make.

She made a choice: to give birth to her baby and provide it with loving, responsible, surrogate parents. Her daughter was born July 7, 1991. Before giving the baby to the adoptive parents, Vicky had a dedication ceremony for the child.

Today Vicky is attending the university and is finding God's help in building a meaningful, happy life. "This angel of mine has given me something that is irreplaceable," she observes.

In Vicky's case, the angel appeared and the message about her unborn child was given in a dream. Two thousand years earlier, an angel appeared to a man named Joseph in a dream (Luke 1:20) with instructions about another unborn child, who was to be called Jesus. Later, in Matthew 2:13, the angel appeared again to Joseph in a dream warning him that Herod was going to search for Jesus to kill him. Joseph acted on the message given by the angel. Joseph had no doubt about the reality of the angel even in a dream. Vicky as well was so profoundly moved that she does not doubt that she was visited by an angel with a message from God.

Our English word *angel* comes from the Greek, the language in which the New Testament was written. The original meaning of the word was *messenger*. When a person reads the Bible in Greek, the word for *angel* can mean either a person who is a messenger or a heavenly being.

Many times in the Scripture, God used angels to give his message. An angel told Mary that she would be the mother of Jesus. An angel announced the Resurrection on the first Easter. An angel gave instructions to the disciples when Jesus ascended into heaven. In both the Old and New Testaments angels are used to give God's messages in matters of great importance, or more personal, private details. Since this was a major activity of angels in biblical times, it is no surprise that God still uses them today.

"Many people have shared with us how God used an angel to give them a specific message. This chapter contains a brief sampling of angels' giving information that otherwise would not have been known.

Four Angels Dressed in Black

From early childhood, Marilynn Carlson Webber, one of the authors of this book, has had an interest in angels. She confides that she had always wanted to see an angel—if not in person, at least in a dream. That never happened until the summer of 1993. Marilynn relates her unexpected experience.

"Four angels came to me in a dream, but they were not the glorious, shining angels I had always pictured in my mind's eye. I was startled to see that they were dressed in black. Their body language spoke volumes. They were in mourning. Summoning up my courage, I asked, 'Why are you in mourning?'

"One angel replied, 'Because you are dying. If something is not done soon, you will die.'

"Suddenly I was wide awake. I was frightened by the vividness of my dream. I was trembling because of the encounter. For the first time, I also felt pain—severe pain.

"I woke my husband. 'I need to tell you my dream,' I insisted to my sleepy spouse. 'It's so real. I know that God sent his angels with a message.'

"I described the black-robed angels in mourning and

their message that I was dying unless something was done . . . soon.

" 'First thing in the morning,' Bill told me, 'we will find a doctor.'

"I had not seen a doctor for a few years. I had my excuses. My internist had retired. I had gone to two other doctors, but although they were comparatively young, both had stopped practicing medicine. The last physician warned me that I needed to be monitored for cancer and had recommended a specialist, but when I called for an appointment I was told that he was taking no new patients. I had meant to find another doctor but for two years had put it off.

"The morning after my dream my husband urgently called the doctor that had been recommended. The receptionist told him the doctor was still taking no new patients. Bill asked to talk to the doctor himself but was transferred to his nurse. He told the nurse that his wife needed to see the doctor immediately. When she asked why it was so urgent, he told her of the dream.

" 'It's impossible for you to see Dr. King,' the nurse replied, 'but let me see if I can work you in to see one of his colleagues.'

"In a minute she came back on the line. 'I have an appointment for your wife with Dr. Keeney,' she said. 'He is one of the best oncologists in the area.'

"With fear and trembling I kept my appointment with Dr. Keeney. As he took my medical history, he asked what had brought me to see him. I poured out my dream about four angels dressed in black and watched as he wrote it in my file.

"A biopsy was taken, then almost every known medical test—or at least it seemed to be that way to me. There *was* cancer and a tumor that needed to be removed. Dr. Keeney explained that pain was not a symptom of this type of cancer. Why, then, had I felt pain on the night of my dream? I believe that God knew that I was a reluctant patient, and to get my attention he needed not only to send his angels in a dream but also to underscore their message with pain.

"As a part of the routine preoperative procedure I was seen by a resident. He began taking a complete medical history. I asked why it was necessary inasmuch as I had answered the same questions for Dr. Keeney. He replied that Dr. Keeney was the best in his field, he could remember everything about all his patients, but that no one could read his handwriting. 'All I can make out in your medical history is that four angels in mourning came to you in a dream and told you that you were dying if nothing was done.'

"Surgery was set for September 2 at the Loma Linda University Medical Center. The doctor told me I was considered to be a high-risk patient. I believe in prayer and began to ask my friends to pray for me. I asked to be put on every prayer chain I knew.

"The day of surgery came. The doctor told my husband that he could expect me to be in intensive care for two days. Surgery took four hours, but after a few hours' stay in the recovery room, I was placed in a regular hospital room. Five days later I returned home. Prayers are answered!

"The doctor explained they had caught the cancer in time and were able to remove it completely. I did not need chemotherapy or any follow-up treatments, but if the cancer had not been discovered it would have spread and been life-threatening.

"I knew I would have put it off, as I had done for years, but God, in his mercy, sent four angels in mourning, dressed in black, to impress me with the urgency of seeing the doctor. I continue to praise God for his goodness and my health!"

An Angel Appeared to Mary in a Dream

Bad things do happen to good people. In this instance it happened to a young lawyer. Richard Boden was working hard to represent his clients, building a reputation as an honest, fully competent attorney. Suddenly his world came crashing down when his senior law partner suffered a complete breakdown. To Richard's dismay, he found that his partner had made many unwise decisions about which Richard had known nothing. Now he found that he was responsible for debts that were not of his making and that it was necessary to dissolve the partnership.

To put it simply, he was without a job in a time when the market was flooded with lawyers. For every opening there would be a hundred applicants. Beginning his own practice would be costly, and Richard was wiped out financially because of his partner's irresponsibility. To become a partner in a firm usually requires a sizable investment. By now Richard had two small children, a house, and obligations. How would he be able to begin again? Both Rich and Mary prayed for guidance in what seemed to be an impossible situation.

Rich showed Mary an ad in the *Daily Law Journal*. It gave few details, not even the name of the firm, only asking for resumés to be sent to a post-office box in Redlands, California, a town nearby. Mary said, "Why don't you respond to it? You don't know what it might be. You are a good attorney with a very good reputation."

Richard explained, "Honey, even if it is a good position and they want me, no one would accept me if I don't have money to buy into a partnership. But probably it's an opening for a beginning law clerk, and the salary is so low that we wouldn't be able to meet our obligations. Besides, if I were to work in Redlands, there is probably only one firm I would be interested in, and I know that would be impossible." Mary accepted that.

That night Mary had a dream. It was no ordinary dream—it was forceful, compelling. She heard a voice saying, "You are to tell Rich to answer that ad. This is the direction you are to take. It will lead to blessing."

In the morning Mary remembered the dream vividly. She had never had a dream affect her so deeply. Certainly she was not used to hearing voices, whether she was awake or asleep. Instinctively she knew that it was an angel giving her this message. She shared her dream with Richard and urged him to answer the ad, but Richard was so certain that the opening must be for a poorly paid entry-level position that he did not feel it was worth the time to apply.

A few nights later the angel spoke to Mary again in a dream. The message was clear. It was so strong. "Do not continue with what you are doing. You are to answer the ad. When you answer the ad, you will receive the right kind of response, and it will be a blessing." Mary woke up, stirred to the depth of her being.

"Richard," she exclaimed, "I just had this dream, and I was told to tell you that you are supposed to answer that ad."

Richard sleepily replied, "Honey, you just want me to do this, and you're just thinking that it will be a simple answer to our problems."

Mary replied, "Hon, I just can't tell you how strongly I feel. This is a clear message from God, and this is something we must do. It can't hurt."

"All right," Richard agreed reluctantly.

He sent his resumé on Thursday morning. On Friday

afternoon he received a call from the firm—the only firm he said that he would be interested in. Richard listened in amazement as they offered him a full partnership with no money going into it. On Monday the details were worked out. On Tuesday morning Rich moved into his new office and began work.

For the first few months Richard brought in no business, but the firm paid his full salary. It was unbelievable. As time went by, Richard became an important partner and paid back the salary that he had been given in the first few months.

After he was well-established, Richard asked, "Why? Why did you take me into the firm? You are all such good businessmen, and this was not an attractive business proposition to take me in when I had no funds to invest in the firm."

The partners looked at each other. "We don't know why," they replied. "We knew you were a good attorney. We knew your reputation was outstanding. But we don't know why. We've never done that before."

Richard and Mary know. It was God who turned the hearts and minds of the law partners. It was the Lord who was taking care of them in the most difficult time of their lives. And Mary will always remember how the angel came to her in a dream with God's clear message.

The Case of the Missing Briefcase

It had been a thrilling day, thought Ken Churchill, pastor of the Minnetonka Community Church, as he stood in the boarding area of the Minneapolis-St. Paul International Airport. He and fifteen members of the church youth group had just had prayer with John and Carolyn Quam. The Quams were members of their church and were leaving for their first term as missionaries to Brazil. The pastor and the youth group watched as the new missionaries crossed the tarmac, climbed the steps, and entered the plane. As the door of the airliner closed, everyone left the gate area except the church group. "Let's stay until they take off," suggested the pastor.

John and Carolyn boarded the aircraft and found their seats. Carolyn held the baby as John stowed their carry-on luggage. Suddenly John froze. "What's wrong?" asked his wife, apprehensively.

"My briefcase," John answered, his voice filled with apprehension. "It's not here. Have you seen it?"

"Not since we boarded the plane," Carolyn replied. She joined the search, but it was clear: The briefcase was not there.

A stewardess came down the aisle. "Please take your seats and fasten your seat belts," she said. "We will soon be preparing for take-off."

"I need your help," John implored. "I left my briefcase in the airport. It has our passports, our tickets, and our money. We can't go to Brazil without it."

It was against procedures, but the stewardess arranged to open the door. John almost jumped down the stairs, rushed across the tarmac and into the waiting room. It was deserted except for the church group. "Quick, help me!" the missionary called to them urgently. "I have to find my briefcase. It has all our passports, tickets, and all our money. It must be here somewhere."

Frantically the group searched the boarding area. There was no briefcase. As they searched, they prayed for help.

"You are looking for a briefcase," a voice said quietly. Everyone stopped and looked at the speaker. They had been alone, but here was a stranger, a woman about in her mid-thirties, dressed in a suit. Who was she? Where had she come from?

"Your briefcase is not here," she continued calmly. "It is in the main terminal, in the middle of the floor."

Quam and Churchill took off at a run down the deserted concourse. As they entered the main terminal, they saw the briefcase standing in the middle of the floor. John grabbed the briefcase, turned, ran back up the concourse, past the cheering youth group, across the tarmac, up the stairs, and into the aircraft. Seconds later the door closed, and the pilot began to leave the gate.

Pastor Churchill walked back up the concourse, praising God for answered prayer. He joined the jubilant youth group at the waiting room. Pastor Churchill had thanked God; now there was one other to thank. He looked for the woman who had told them where the briefcase was. She was not there. He asked the youth group, "Where did the woman go that told us where to find the briefcase?" No one had seen her leave. And where could she have gone? The gate was at the end of the concourse. There was no other outside door. If she had gone down the concourse to the terminal, she would have had to pass Quam and Churchill. They saw no one.

"I know it was an angel," Churchill says confidently. "There is no other explanation."

John Quam now heads Concerts of Prayer, an international prayer organization based in Minneapolis. "We often see God work through unexplained circumstances," he declares. "God does answer prayer. And when necessary, God sends his angels."

An Urgent Wake-Up Message

When Megan Richmond was very small, about a year old, she had an ear infection and ran a high fever, a real concern for her parents. Her tiny body was shaken by the high temperature. Later, the little girl fell out of the car and injured her head. The doctors performed all kinds of examinations and tests on the young child and found that her brain-wave pattern was very abnormal.

The doctors reported that Megan would never be able to function normally and would not be able to concentrate. Explaining that high fevers were dangerous for this small patient, the doctor prescribed medications to be used to reduce fevers. Megan's mother, Jill, kept the medicine ready for use in the linen closet near Megan's bedroom.

Later Megan had another earache. Her mother put her to bed, praying that the pain would not keep her child from sleeping.

Jill was wakened from her sleep at about two in the morning by the voice of an angel saying, "Get up!" Jill remembers a nonverbal message. She knew that she was to go to the closet, take the medicine, and hurry to put it under Megan's tongue. Without questioning, Jill quickly gave the medicine to the sleeping child. The mother stayed by her daughter's bedside, wondering why she had been summoned when her daughter seemed to be sleeping without problems. Then her daughter's body was shaken by a major seizure.

"I know that God in his graciousness had sent an angelic messenger to me to give the medicine in time to lower the fever and prevent brain damage in Megan," Jill explains. "If I had not wakened and given her the medicine some time before her seizure began, she probably would have had permanent brain damage.

"It will be interesting to see what Megan does with her life. At this point in time she is in her second year of law school. She was a Phi Beta Kappa at U.S.C. and has won many scholastic awards. We know that she is able to study and concentrate, and we give glory to God for that."

An Angel Named Sly

Six months from the day Katie Lynn Kress was born, she was readmitted to Children's Hospital of Michigan for open-heart surgery, all eleven pounds of her. The surgery was a success. The tiny child's chest looked like a road map of stitches and scars, but she was alive. During her recovery Katie Lynn developed complications with blood clots and a week later was back in surgery. The major surgery began Friday afternoon at 1:30. By 8:30 that night she was returned to the cardiac unit. The surgery was a success, the doctor declared, and the Kress family, exhausted as they were, rejoiced. They thanked God, but their hearts still ached as they saw their little one hooked to seventeen intravenous tubes.

On Saturday the family returned to the hospital to spend time with the brave six-months-old infant. When it came time to leave, Carolyn, the mother, decided to stay with her baby a few more minutes while her husband, Rob, went to get the car. Their son, Ryan, and their daughter, Tiffany, decided to stop at the cafeteria to get a Coke on the way down. They all planned to meet in the hospital lobby.

Rob retrieved the car and was waiting in the lobby for his family. The lobby, usually a busy place, was quiet. For about ten minutes Rob was the only person there. Then a bearded black man wearing a maintenance uniform stepped out from behind a large pillar. "How are you doing, Rob?" he asked, smiling.

A little startled, Rob replied, "Good, how are you?" Rob was not surprised that the stranger called him by name. Rob Kress is the popular weathercaster for channel 7 in Detroit, and strangers often call him by name.

"I hear that your daughter is going home tomorrow," the workman said.

Rob laughed, remembering the sick little girl he had just left. "No, she just had five more hours of surgery yesterday. They say she'll be lucky if she can go home a week from tomorrow."

"I must have misunderstood, then," the worker replied. He leaned against the pillar in his soiled maintenance uniform, a soft smile on his face, as though he knew something that Rob did not know but was too considerate to contradict a burdened father. *There is something different about this man*, Rob thought. A feeling of warmth and kindness seemed to flow from him.

"They call me Sly," he said. "You know, like Sylvester."

Rob looked down for a moment, wondering what was keeping his family so long. When he looked up, he was alone. Sly was nowhere to be seen. There had not been time for him to leave the lobby. The man had simply vanished.

Carolyn came down from the hospital room. Ryan and Tiffany, their Cokes finished, found their father in the lobby. They began the drive home on I-75. Much to his surprise Rob heard himself say, "Katie is coming home tomorrow."

"No way," Carolyn answered. She looked at her husband as if he were out of his mind. "I just talked with the nurses, and they said she will have to be in the hospital for several days."

"Katie will be coming home tomorrow," Rob repeated. His mind knew what the doctors and nurses had said, had seen with his own eyes how very sick Katie was, but in his heart Rob believed.

The following day, Sunday, Rob and Carolyn returned to the hospital about noon. As they walked into the cardiac unit on the sixth floor southwest, Katie's nurse, Audra, looked relieved. "I've been trying to reach you. Katie can go home today."

"What?" Carolyn asked in disbelief.

"When the doctors were making their rounds this morning they examined Katie," the nurse explained. "They found she is remarkably healed and ready to go home."

Rob and Carolyn walked into Katie's room and found her smiling. The intravenous tubes were gone. The pain-reliever drip was no longer taped to her little hand. It was obvious that the little girl no longer had pain. In twenty minutes they were checked out of the hospital and headed home.

Rob knows that the healing came from God. But what about the message that Katie would be going home the next day? When Sly spoke those words, no human had reason to believe it would be possible. The doctors and nurses all were agreed on a much longer time of healing. It wasn't until seven o'clock the next morning that the doctors knew that she had been healed.

And what about the messenger, Sly—? "I have no doubt that he was an angel," Kress says. What did he do? "The only thing he did was bring me good news. Katie Lynn is so little and so innocent, yet so radiant. We still have some big bumps in the road ahead of us, but I'm positive that everything will be well. Thank you, Lord, and thank you, Sly."

A Mother's Midnight Message

Cindy was very, very sick. Throughout second grade she had repeated bouts with strep throat. "This is very serious," her doctor warned her mother, Laurel Hammond. "When she recovers, if she has strep throat one more time you will probably lose your daughter."

Laurel had been sitting by her daughter's bedside for days. Cindy was lifeless. Her body was white. The child just lay there, very, very sick.

The mother kept her vigil into the early morning hours, constantly praying, "Lord, heal my child. Show me what to do. Please heal my Cindy."

Her prayer was interrupted by a soft, kindly voice. It sounded like a woman's voice—loving, confident, caring. "It will be all right. She'll be better in the morning."

Laurel looked around the room for the source of the voice, but she was alone with her sleeping child. There was no one else there. It was three o'clock in the morning, and there was just Laurel sitting next to the bed, holding her daughter's hand. She recognized that it was a message from an angel. She knew that her daughter would recover. The mother fell asleep on the floor by her sick child.

About seven in the morning the little girl woke up. "I feel better, Mom," Cindy said. "I'm hungry. Can I get up now?"

Cindy recovered completely. Her doctor took precautionary measures, did a culture of every child in her classroom, and discovered the child who was the carrier. That child was treated and was healed also.

No Well-Deserved Spanking
by Esther "Robbe" Roberts

"When I was about three years old, we lived in a two-story apartment house on Lemon street in Marietta, Georgia. One day I was playing in our small front yard. Mother was upstairs in our apartment making a new pinafore and blouse for me to wear to church on Easter Sunday. Mother had an old treadle-type Singer sewing machine that someone had given her. I remember marveling at how fast she could pedal that old machine when creating outfits for the entire family.

"I also remember thinking about how pretty I would be in my brand-new, red-and-white-striped pinafore. I was so busy thinking about my new outfit that I forgot Mother's instructions never to play in the street.

"When Mother came running out of the front door, that's exactly where she found me—sitting in the middle of the street, playing!

"To my surprise, instead of getting a well-deserved spanking, Mother grabbed me up into her arms and hugged me close to her bosom. I thought for a moment that she was even going to cry.

"As Mother carried me up the stairs, she kept repeating, 'Thank you, Lord, thank you, Lord.' Well, even as a three-year-old I began to think that mother was behaving somewhat strangely. At that moment we heard a loud, rumbling noise coming from the street. Mother, still carrying me, rushed over to our window just in time for us to see a big dump truck speeding away out of sight.

"Mother's eyes were happy with joy when she turned to me and said, 'God's angel told me you were in the street and to hurry before it was too late!'

"That Easter Sunday, while wearing my new, red-and-white-striped pinafore and blouse, I remember thinking about how glad I was that God's angel and my mother loved me."

Snake in the Manger

It has been years since Opal Housley was a girl living on a farm near Inola, Oklahoma. One event from her teen years is still as clear as the day it happened.

Opal's father had taken the wagon to town, leaving his wife and daughter to do the chores. Opal went to the barn to get some straw to make a nest for one of the chickens in the henhouse. She was about to reach into the manger for a handful of straw when a voice said clearly, "Stop! There is a snake in the manger."

Opal looked around to see who had spoken. No one was there. She was the only person in the barn. She looked in the manger. It was full of straw. She could see nothing else, certainly not a snake.

Opal stepped closer and started to reach into the manger again. "Stop!" the voice commanded. "There is a snake in the manger." The farm girl froze with her hand in mid-air. Her eyes searched the manger. There was no sign of a snake. She looked around the barn. It was empty. She was alone.

Opal did not know what to think of the voice, but she did know that she needed straw for the nest, and since she could not see a snake in the manger, she decided to get the straw. She reached out the third time. "Stop!" ordered the voice. "Don't touch it. There is a snake in the manger."

"No, there isn't," Opal said out loud, but she stood, looking into the manger. Slowly the straw began to move. First Opal saw the eyes, then the head of the snake.

She ran for the farmhouse and returned with her mother. The snake was still in the manger when they arrived. "It's a poisonous snake!" Opal's mother exclaimed. "It probably came up from the pond. What a close call you had."

Then with the skill that farmers' wives have demonstrated throughout history, Opal's mother quickly killed the snake. Together the two thanked God for the warning that had saved her life.

Chapter
12

The Cleansing Angel

In prison, Otis realized that he would be behind bars for years. He knew that he had made wrong choices, that he was guilty, that he had caused others to suffer. Now he was suffering.

It wasn't just the confinement of prison, although that was suffering indeed. Even worse were the thoughts that kept returning. Otis could not avoid them, day or night. He had caused injury to others; he had been wrong; he had sinned; he felt dirty. Otis felt more than remorse— he was tormented with guilt and despair.

All these feelings flooded over Otis as he lay on his prison bunk, longing for peace but feeling only anguish. Whenever he tried to change his thoughts, the old hurts continued to haunt him.

In desperation, Otis began to pray the prayer of a man who had hit absolute bottom. Tears streamed down his face from the hurt within. He felt filthy, as though his entire body was filled with the dirt of sin.

Suddenly the prisoner felt a strange supernatural presence within his cell. As he lay on his bunk, he felt a large hand, the hand of an angel going into his mouth, down his throat, deep within him. Then slowly the hand withdrew, bringing with it all the dirt from within. At first Otis was overcome with a sense of relief, then he felt a new sensation—warm, reassuring, comforting. It was peace! It came like a flood, washing away past guilt and healing painful memories. Otis could not stop crying, but now the tears were those of pure joy. He knew that he would remain in prison for years, but more important—he was cleansed, forgiven, accepted by God.

It was an experience so profound that Otis told only his mother, then later the M-2* visitor who came regularly to see him. Now fourteen years later as he shares his story, Otis is still in prison but retains that inner sense of peace. There are days when he gets discouraged and sad after so many years of being locked up. At those times Otis remembers the time that the angel brought cleansing to his cell, and he prays for the peace to be returned. And God still answers that prayer.

Otis's story seems strange to many. Those who are familiar with the Bible usually see an immediate parallel to Isaiah, chapter 6. Isaiah tells of being in the presence of God. The order of angels known as seraphs were leading in worship using the words, "Holy, holy, holy is the Lord Almighty; the whole earth is full of his glory."

In the presence of God's holiness, Isaiah was overcome with a sense of his own sinfulness. "Woe to me!" he cried. "I am ruined! For I am a man of unclean lips, and I live among a people of unclean lips, and my eyes have seen the King, the Lord Almighty."

Then one of the angels flew to Isaiah with a live coal that he had taken off the altar. He touched Isaiah's mouth and said, "See, this has touched your lips; your guilt is taken away and your sin atoned for."

There are several similar elements in both accounts. There is the overwhelming sense of guilt, a feeling of utter hopelessness. There is the cry to God. Through Scripture the principle is clear that forgiveness of sin comes only from God, but in both stories there is a need for more than forgiveness: There is the need for freedom from guilt. The sinner needs not only to be forgiven but

---

*The M-2 program recruits people who are willing to "adopt" a prisoner and visit him or her regularly.

to *feel* forgiven. There needs to be a symbolic act of cleansing to set the person free.

For Isaiah this cleansing came when an angel touched his lips with a live coal. For Otis it was when the angel reached into the depths of his being, symbolically removing the filth within.

God uses his angels to help Old Testament prophets and present-day prisoners. Angels, when called on by God, minister in the most appropriate way to bring a sense of cleansing, forgiveness, and peace.

Chapter
13

Michael Landon: An Angel Unawares

Mary Dorr has had a long career in radio, television, and as a public speaker. She is the founder of the Angel Awards. The Angel Awards recognize outstanding films, television shows, performers, and other media that promote wholesome values without reliance on violence and sex. She relates an experience that happened at one of the awards dinners. Mary is convinced that an angel was present that evening.

"During a career of more than thirty-five years before the television cameras, any number of times angels have tapped me on the shoulder and led me on paths I would not have otherwise walked.

"I well remember one, about a real-life drama that concerned a ten-year-old girl and Michael Landon as an angel who carried a message to God.

"There is a prelude. Landon was finishing eleven years in *Little House on the Prairie,* and the network was frantic to find another television series for this much-loved and talented actor. The executives told him that they wanted something different from *Bonanza* or *Little House on the Prairie* but with the same heartwarming appeal.

"Michael had an idea. He would portray an angel come down to earth, helping people, solving dramatic situations, doing good, fighting evil, along with a side-kick, Victor French.

"The suggestion appalled the top brass. The viewers

would never accept a macho man like Michael playing an angel. Ridiculous. He was out of his mind.

"He persisted, and *Highway to Heaven* was born and for several years drew high ratings. Not only did viewers accept him, but they loved him in the role. What the network hadn't foreseen was that he was such a talented writer as well as an actor—that he could make it all credible.

"We skip now to the International Angel Awards that I founded and produced for seventeen years. We honored *Highway to Heaven* with a Gold Angel for the inspiration as well as the entertainment that the show had brought to millions the world over.

"The next year we presented a Gold Angel to Michael himself. The evening that he came to the banquet ceremony at the Regent Beverly Wilshire hotel in Beverly Hills, I was rushing about trying to meet head-on all of the crises that pop up at every Awards dinner.

"Although harried, I noticed a little girl about ten, with a sweet face, standing outside on the street along with many others, mostly teenagers, who were waiting to get autographs from the arriving celebrities. Every time a limousine pulled up, she would crane her neck but never asked for an autograph. The crowd was noisy; she was quiet. Obviously, she was alone and, I thought, awfully young to be by herself.

"Apprehensive, I stepped out into the street. 'Are you waiting for your parents?' She had a sad, drawn, old-for-her-years face. She was neatly but inexpensively dressed in a blue cotton with white daisies spotted about.

"'No, ma'am,' she said politely. 'I'm waiting for Mr. Landon. I have to see him. I must. I have to.'

"There was desperation in her voice. Then I noticed her clenched hands.

" 'He's already here. Having dinner. If you want an autograph . . .'

" 'No, no. But I've got to talk with him. Just for a minute. I promise, I won't take longer. I won't be a nuisance. Please . . .'

" 'What do you want to see him about?'

"She was struggling to hold back the tears. I couldn't make out what she was saying. Not that it mattered. Never in all my career had I ever permitted anyone to interfere with celebrities when they were having dinner. It was a cardinal rule of mine. (Once I had fought off a pack of children closing in on Randy Travis.)

"Then an angel nudged me. It *had* to have been an angel. Who else or what else could it have been? Against my will, I found myself taking her hot little hand, and then we were walking through the vast ballroom crowded with milling people to Michael Landon's table. He was laughing and talking with friends. He had come this night directly from a television set where he had been working since 6:00 A.M. He was bound to be exhausted.

" 'Forgive me,' I said, hesitantly. I didn't recognize my voice because it was not I who was talking—it was that blasted angel who had gotten me into this situation. 'I have a very desperate little girl . . .'

"He turned about smiling. 'Hi,' he said.

"She was up against him immediately, whispering frantically into his ear. The smile vanished, and his eyes darkened. He was nodding. He looked about. 'Somebody got a scrap of paper?' He was handed a blank note sheet and was writing on it. I could see her name scrawled, an address, a phone number.

"He took her to him in a bear hug. She managed a smile and thanked him, then hugged me, and was gone.

" 'Her little brother's dying,' he said to me. 'Of cancer. She didn't know what kind.'

"He said nothing more, and I didn't ask. After all, this was confidential between a little girl and an 'angel' taking a message to God.

"Maybe he phoned her brother. Maybe he sent a toy. Undoubtedly, he got a message through to God. Knowing Michael Landon, he was a truly great angel unawares.

"And then there was the angel who had made it all possible. The one who had nudged me and pushed me. That angel was not all sweetness and light. He was determined that I give that little girl a chance to talk with Michael Landon.

"Don't tell me that there are not angels roaming about."

Do Angels Really Sing?

Some people who thrive on trivia love to point out that there is no mention in the Bible of angels singing. They point out that even in the Christmas story the Bible says, "Suddenly a great company of the heavenly host appeared with the angel, praising God and saying, 'Glory to God in the highest, and on earth peace to men on whom his favor rests'" (Luke 2:13).

While it is true that the verse uses the word *saying* instead of *singing*, most people find it more logical to imagine the angels singing a great "Gloria" rather than acting as a speech choir. And doesn't "praising" God imply singing, as well?

We do find the angels singing in Job 38:7. Talking about the time of creation, the Lord says ... "the morning stars sang together/and all the angels shouted for joy." Most biblical scholars agree that in this passage the term *morning stars* is another name for *angels*. This is an example of parallelism in Hebrew poetry, where the second line states the same idea as the first line.

The apostle John heard angels sing. He wrote in Revelation 5:9 about the angels: "And they sang a new song." Perhaps one reason that people do not recognize this as angels singing is that the words *living creatures* ("beasts" in the King James) and *elders* are used. Chapter four of Revelation clearly describes the elders and living creatures as angels.

In Revelation 5:11 we read, "Then I looked and heard the voice of many angels, numbering thousands upon thousands, and ten thousand times ten thousand. They encircled the throne and the living creatures and the elders. In a loud voice they sang:

'Worthy is the Lamb, who was slain,
to receive power and wealth and wisdom and
    strength
and honor and glory and praise!' "

What a song that must have been!

Do angels sing today? Here are a few recent stories of those who have heard them.

Songs My Mother Taught Me

When Lois Ponte was growing up, her mother, Marian Fleming, often told her the story of the day the angels sang. As a child, it was Lois's favorite story. It still is today.

When Marian Fleming was a young wife, she fell down icy cement steps, seriously injuring herself. Worse than the physical pain, which was intense, was the young woman's despair. She knew that there was a possibility that she wouldn't walk again. She had three little children—how would she possibly cope?

Then one day as she lay alone in her bed, music filled her room—the sweetest singing she'd ever heard. She looked around to see if anyone was there even though she knew that no one was. Still the sweet music continued. The words wound around her, filling her with peace. She'd never heard the song before, but its words were comforting and sung with otherworldly certainty and love.

As the music continued, Marian's despair was turned to trust. She knew that she was hearing angels—singing and encouraging her. That song renewed the courage and determination that she needed to fight her way back to health.

Only after she was walking again did she see and recognize in a hymnal the unfamiliar song she'd heard sung. Excitedly, she traced the words: "God will take care of you, through every day, o'er all the way ..." It became her favorite song because she knew for a fact that the lyrics were credible.

Long after she was walking again, Marian kept these things and pondered them in her heart. Every once in a while, she'd tell her story to her enraptured children.

Many years later, as Marian lay dying in the hospital, her daughter Lois would sit by her bedside and sing "God Will Take Care of You." She hoped that her mother, though in a coma, could hear it and that it would be a loving bridge between this world and the next as the angels took up the final chorus.

Cherie Hanson and the Complimentary Neighbors

One fall evening the Hanson family had a strange experience: They heard angels singing around their house. In awe they listened to the incredible music all evening long. They couldn't help wondering if they were sharing some wonderful dream. The next morning, their unbelieving neighbors commented on their beautiful singing the night before. "We had no idea that you folks are so talented," they commented. "We've never heard anyone with such amazing voices!"

Says Cherie, "It was then we knew that what we'd heard had been real and not a dream. God is great!"

Laurel Hammond—Singing Alleluia

Laurel Hammond was singing as she drove to work. Instead of letting the traffic annoy her, she preferred to praise God. This morning the traffic was low, driving was easy, and Laurel was especially happy. Thinking of God's love, Laurel began to sing, "Alleluia, alleluia!"

She became aware that others were singing with her— but she was alone in the car. Laurel checked her radio. It was off.

As she began to sing again, her car was filled with glorious harmony. The unseen voices had a soft, light, ethereal quality. As Laurel sang her alleluias, the unseen voices added harmonies different from any she had heard. The sheer beauty of their voices seemed to urge Laurel to lift her voice in renewed praise. When she stopped, the voices became fainter and slowly faded away.

"But I heard them!" Laurel exclaims. "It was such a blessing, such a confirmation from God."

Jill Richmond—the Angels' Song

Jill Richmond and her friend Linda were planning a "Life in the Spirit" seminar for their parish in Orange, California. Their lives had been touched by God, and they were excited about sharing with others. Jill had taken the lead in a similar seminar that had been well-received. Linda had been her "gofer," working largely behind the scenes, making sure that everything needed was ready and when it was needed, to "go fer" what was necessary.

In the next seminar Linda would be the leader, and Jill would be her "gofer." The two had been planning and praying; now they decided that the time had come to share their plans with the pastor and ask his counsel. They came to the church and rang the doorbell. Jill and Linda waited. They rang the doorbell again, and waited . . . and waited . . . and waited. The two friends were talking as they waited. Then Linda said, "Jill, do you hear what I hear?"

"Yes!" replied Jill. "It's *angels* singing!"

It was as though the heavens had opened up and the two girls could hear through the opening the angels singing glory to God. The two women had come to glorify God's name. They stood in the entry of the church, bathed in the beauty of the celestial music, their hearts caught up in the sense of worship. The music became softer, then faded away. When the music stopped, Jill and Linda quietly left the church. Their visit had been completely rewarding. There was no disappointment that there had been no one to open the church door, for the heavens had opened. There had been no words of pastoral counsel, but they had shared in the praises of God as sung by the angels. Their prayers had been answered in an unexpected way, their lives had been blessed, and they were renewed in their service to God.

Chapter
15

Angels at the Time of Death

When Elijah died, a chariot of fire and horses of fire appeared, and Elijah went up to heaven in a whirlwind (2 Kings 11). What a way to go! But what does an ordinary Christian have to look forward to? Something just as exciting, according to Jesus.

Lazarus was neither a prophet nor a religious leader of any kind. He was a beggar covered with sores. The time came when the beggar died and was carried by the angels to heaven, Jesus taught in Luke 16:22. It wasn't that the angels were just with him—they *carried* him! We have it on the authority of Jesus himself that God sends his angels for us as we end this earthly life and begin eternal life in heaven.

Sometimes as death draws near, a person catches a glimpse of the angels and glory beyond. That was the experience of Stephen, recorded in Acts 7. Since that time, down through church history, there have been many reliable accounts of people who have seen angels and the glory of God at the time of death.

When D. L. Moody was dying, he said, "Earth recedes, and heaven opens before me. This is no dream . . . it is beautiful. There is no valley here. God is calling me, and I must go."

Billy Graham tells of the death of his maternal grandmother. The room seemed to fill with a heavenly light. She sat up in bed and almost laughingly said, "I see Jesus. He has his arms outstretched toward me.

"I see Ben (her husband who had died some years

earlier) and I see the angels." Then her life left her, and she was absent from the body but present with the Lord.

This kind of experience is not unusual. Many, many people have related firsthand accounts of observing the presence of angels at the time of the death of a loved one. Sometimes only the dying person sees God's angels. In some instances other people who are in the room also see the angels. Often there is a bright light that fills the room. Other times it is in one place, and its movement appears to be that of an angel in the form of light.

Why is it that not everyone has this experience? Today many people die in the hospital, often sedated. It may be that the drugs keep many from being aware of and reporting what is happening to them. But although the appearance of angels before death has happened frequently through history, it has never been something that has happened indiscriminately to all. Apparently God has his reasons for allowing some persons to experience angels shortly before death—perhaps one reason is to encourage and comfort those loved ones who are present.

Psalm 116:15 tells us that "Precious in the sight of the LORD is the death of His saints." What better time for the ministry of angels than during the "graduation" of God's people from one life to the next? Cheryl Wilson tells a beautiful story about her own experience with death.

Cheryl Wilson—Angel at Her Side

In 1970 Cheryl and Larry Wilson were a young, married, missionary couple stationed in the little town of Jacnel, Haiti. Today there are modern roads, but in 1970 there were none. It was a rough, day's journey to Port-au-Prince, the only "modern" city.

Life in Jacnel was simple and without modern conveniences. There was no refrigeration—anything that would spoil had to be eaten the day it was brought home from the open-air market. There were no modern medical facilities at all.

Sadly, while they were there, Cheryl suffered a miscarriage. Larry got her to Port-au-Prince, where she was placed under a doctor's care. She returned to Jacnel when it seemed that she had recovered.

But back home in Jacnel, Cheryl began to hemorrhage. Larry and Cheryl's mother, who was visiting, tried their best to care for her. They knew there was no way that she would survive the rough trip back to Port-au-Prince.

By the second day, a Sunday, the hemorrhaging became even more severe. Cheryl didn't want Larry to worry about her because she knew that he had Sunday services to think about. As her condition worsened, she pulled herself out of bed to try to get to the bathroom.

In the hall, weakened from the severe loss of blood, she fell. Larry and her mother heard her fall and came running. He picked her up and carried her back to her bed.

Larry held Cheryl close to him, willing her back to life, but it was too late. She died in his arms. Larry says that he knew the moment her heart and her breathing stopped and her spirit departed, but he continued to cradle her body as it turned cold and ashen gray, crying and praying that God would have mercy and please return her to him. He loved and needed her so much.

Cheryl was having a much different experience.

As she looked up from the bed, she saw a "beautiful, glorious" angel in the upper corner of the room. He was bathed in light. He held out his hand to her and said, "Peace I give unto you."

Cheryl felt herself float up, out of her body toward the magnificent being. For a moment she looked back and saw herself lying in her husband's arms, and saw her mother sitting there, begging the Lord to bring her back. Then, with the angel close beside her, she continued floating up beyond the confining bonds of earth, in a radiant, glorious place. There she saw a river—not an earthly river but a heavenly river—pouring from above from the direction the angel was taking her. There were people in the river, and they were shouting and praising and worshiping God in a language unbound by earthly words.

As Cheryl and the angel progressed upward, the light became more and more brilliant, and Cheryl knew that they were approaching the Father's throne. She couldn't see upward because of the blinding light, but below her she could still see the people rejoicing and praising. She was filled to overflowing with joy and love and peace. The radiance that surrounded and filled her was beyond her wildest imagining.

From the light above her, Cheryl heard the Lord speak. He said, "I am not finished with your life yet."

As the words were spoken, Cheryl felt herself jerked back down into her body.

On earth, Cheryl had been gone for many minutes—it seemed to Larry like half an hour although he hadn't watched the clock. Larry and Cheryl's mother were stunned by the miracle of Cheryl's return to life. Their tears of grief turned to joy.

But as much as Cheryl loved her family, she wasn't happy to be back. In fact, she wept for days, not from physical pain but from her intense longing to return to the unspeakable love and joy she had known in the presence of the Lord.

Speaking to the Wilsons today, more than twenty years later, you know that they will never forget that day in Haiti. Larry's voice is still laced with anguish when he speaks of holding his dead wife. And Cheryl's voice is still filled with awe and wonder as she describes her journey to heaven. After her experience she read with joy about "the river of the water of life, sparkling like crystal, and coming from the throne of God," which the apostle John had also seen and reported in Revelation 22.

Cheryl says that dying has changed her life. She tries to spend every day praising God with her actions and words and has no fear at all of dying. She knows that what Paul said is true: To live is Christ, to die is gain.

Peggy Gray—Not Alone

The prophet Isaiah describes the Messiah as "a man of sorrows and acquainted with grief," thus it seems only natural that God cares so profoundly for his earthly children who are experiencing loss.

Peggy Gray was mourning the loss of her husband of forty years. One of the hardest things for her was being solitary after so many years of company. One day as she "worked out," she suddenly knew that someone was in the room with her. She turned her head quickly and saw a blinding, bright light—and a very tall figure—just behind her. As she turned, it moved very quickly toward the living room.

Peggy says that the most amazing thing was that she wasn't at all afraid but, in fact, was filled with peace. When she reached the living room, no one was there. After that experience she no longer has felt that she's "living alone." She knows that God is with her, and she's living—and working out!—in the presence of the angels.

Elizabeth O'Donnell—
His Angels Are Flaming Fires

Elizabeth O'Donnell's youngest son John died suddenly in September 1988. His bereaved mother, Elizabeth, mourned her loss and looked for a way to find comfort. John's treasure was his first car, a new Camaro. Elizabeth had begun to drive John's car because driving it made her feel closer to him. She knew that he would have wanted her to use it.

On a beautiful November evening in Southern California, twilight had just fallen when Elizabeth and her daughter Lori returned from shopping. Lori took some grocery bags from the trunk of the car and brought them into the house.

Suddenly a ball of whirling light came from behind Elizabeth, hovered over her head, then moved slowly about ten feet off the ground. She blinked her eyes in disbelief, but the light remained. About five inches in diameter and very intense, it rotated as it moved slowly toward John's car, and paused above it. That seemed to be significant for Elizabeth. She followed the swirling mass of energy as it made its way slowly toward the stairs at the front of their house, then as it went toward the brush-covered hills. Just as suddenly as it had appeared, it vanished.

"I knew that it was an incredibly special event," Elizabeth said. "I took a deep breath and the most wonderful feeling came over me. I had a wonderful sense of peace about my son."

Because Elizabeth has a scientific, inquiring mind, she went to the library to research what she had seen. In all the books she found no clue as to any natural phenomena that resembled what she had seen. She decided just to bask in the wonderful, warm feeling that she was experiencing.

Later a dear friend, Linda Moore, gave her a book about angels. "I found my experience described there," Elizabeth explains. "A ball of whirling energy is one of the forms in which angels can appear to us! An angel encounter? That seems more probable than anything my research uncovered."

Opal Thompson—the Journal

When her adult daughter was diagnosed with cancer, Opal Thompson began her journal. With all her heart she believed it was to be the chronicle of a miracle. Opal read daily the promise of Jesus in John 14:13–14: "I will do whatever you ask in my name, so that the Son may bring glory to the Father. You may ask me for anything in my name, and I will do it."

Opal knew what her daughter, Debbie, was facing. She also knew the power of God, therefore she believed that Deb would be well again. In time, her journal would record not one but three miracles, quite different from what Opal expected. With Opal's permission, we share the following, based on her journal. . . .

"That tiny, wiggly little bundle of trusting love was placed gently in my waiting arms by a smiling nurse. Oh! What a beautiful and special day—February 23, 1953. Then the nurse walked away, and I was alone with my newborn baby. A quiet, overwhelming awe shuddered my body as I began to realize that a living soul, a never-ending soul, had been entrusted to me to care for. I was suddenly frightened. A soul—a person who would never die, would live forever—with or without God— had been born to me to nurture. I clutched her, and pleaded with God to show me how to raise her, and then and there, I returned her to God in full dedication realizing that she had been 'loaned' to her earthly father and me but would always belong to her heavenly Father.

"I knew that for God to show me how to raise her, I would need to know him better. I went to church, joined, and dedicated my life to God. I began a spiritual journey—growing by leaps and bounds in faith and trust—so much so that when the shocking 'sentence of sure death'—CANCER—was announced (twenty-four months maximum), I knew without a doubt that Debbie would be healed. Resting on John 14:13–14, 'I will do whatever you ask in my name so that the Son may bring glory to the Father. You may ask me for anything in my name, and I will do it.' I expected a miracle for Debbie and her family. This is what I believed was God's plan.

"I believed that God would use her healing to bring others to salvation. This he indeed did, for through her two years of illness many people, as a result of witnessing the combined faith of mother and daughter, began to turn to Christ and to experience changed lives. They could see no anger in us toward God, no blaming or turning from him or his plan, no doubts that everything would be all right. Instead they witnessed a positive, joyous attitude that can only be explained by complete faith in Christ.

"Thus it seemed that others had received miracles in their own lives. As the twenty-four-months deadline neared, I awaited my miracle.

" 'Ask me for anything in my name and I will do it' had carried me through thus far; now when would the ultimate miracle be fulfilled? 'For my thoughts are not your thoughts, neither are your ways my ways,' declares the Lord. 'As the heavens are higher than the earth, so are my ways higher than your ways and my thoughts than your thoughts' " (Isaiah 55:8–9). So I was asking God for my miracle, but he was ready to reveal unexpected miracles to me—more beautiful and unbelievable than the changing cells in the human body.

"God knew that with my finite, human limitations I would not be able to see his way. So, through Debbie, he graciously and lovingly allowed me glimpses of his miracles. God gave these heavenly encounters in a timely way to reveal to me this glorious plan.

The First Miracle

"One night in early 1984, I received a phone call from Deb at the hospital at about 12:30 A.M. For two years I had spent nights at the hospital with Deb when she was critical, or when she just needed me. At this time she was doing fine alone most nights. I would go to bed at home with the understanding that she would call me anytime she needed me. The phone would only ring once, and I would always grab it.

"One particular night Deb said that she didn't know what was wrong, she hated to wake me but felt very nervous. I told her that I was on my way, which meant that within twelve minutes I would be there. Before I could hang up, she said that the lights were supposed to go out in the hospital. I knew that the hospital had been on emergency power that day, so I assumed that the lights off had something to do with the earlier problem.

I told Deb to put Angie, her nurse, on the phone. She did I asked Angie what was going on. The nurse told me that the lights would be off for a short time and that they had flashlights to use. I told her to tell Deb that I was on the way. Then Angie said, 'The electricity has gone off now. I can't explain it. There are no lights except in Debbie's room.'

"I hung up and rushed for the hospital. As I topped the hill and rounded the corner on Barton Road, I could see the tower of the Loma Linda University Medical Center, where Deb was on the top floor. An astonishing sight met my eyes. The hospital tower—*except* room 9208— was pitch black from the ground to floor nine. The light from Debbie's room shone like a beacon coming from an otherwise dark tower. How could all the electricity be off except in one room? As I talked with others, I learned that this was physically impossible. The transformers were out for replacement. It was a miracle—a mystery— that the nurses on floor nine were all amazed to see.

"Being a frequent visitor, I knew practically everyone in the hospital, yet it was with some difficulty I persuaded the security guard to let me make my way through the darkened hospital to my daughter's room. Deb was anxious. It was important to her to talk with her mother. She was unable to put into words the anxiety she felt that night, and she needed assurance. At the time of great stress God had sent a sign: Her room stayed bright when all the hospital went dark. We did not understand what it meant. It left us with an awesome, sobering, quiet, indescribable feeling, but we knew this was a sign from God. He was here—in room 9208. In some way we did not yet understand, his will would be done, and his will was good.

The Second Miracle

"One night when Deb was doing fine, she told me that I could go home for the night, and she would call me if she needed me. At 3:00 A.M. the phone rang. The doctor told me that Deb's blood pressure had dropped and she was in danger. She had been taken to a unit on the third floor, where they were working to enhance her blood pressure. When I arrived at the hospital, I learned that Debbie had no blood pressure and had arrested. I was escorted into a semi-dark area. I walked directly to Debbie, took her hand, and said, 'Deb.'

"She opened her eyes and said, 'Mom, what are you doing here? Why are the doctors so upset?' She didn't go into detail at the time, but a few days later she told me what she had meant. A doctor and a nurse had pushed her bed out of the room, down the long hallway to the 9200 elevators. Although Debbie was on the bed in a state of arrest, eyes closed, apparently lifeless, she saw the frantic activity of the doctor and nurse. She heard them trying to reason why there had been this sudden change. She could see herself and the two people running down the hallway, pushing her on her bed. She could not understand why they were so concerned when she felt perfectly fine.

The Third Miracle

"There was a very special time that occurred just before Debbie went into a coma. This event is dear to my heart beyond human expression and pen and paper probably cannot show the depth of it; however, I will try.

"On Thursday, January 12, we all knew that Deb was in trouble. She had been given a massive round of chemotherapy several days earlier and had reached the low point at which all the immune system is gone and the body is sustained through transfusions of the necessary blood, chemicals, and antibiotics.

"I had left the hospital about 5:30 A.M. Jack and Carman had come over to stay with Deb so that I could go home, shower, and go to work. I went back about 8:00 A.M. because I had gotten a call saying that Deb wasn't feeling well. That's all it took, and I was over there.

When I went in and was standing there, Deb said to me, 'Mom, he almost took me, and you weren't here.'

"For a long while I sat by her bed, holding her hand and talking with her in our normal manner. She asked if Ginger was coming over, and I told her yes. I was aware that my daughter was happy; yes, and very peaceful. It was awesome to me. Yet our conversation was completely natural. No one by observing would suspect that in a short time she would be gone.

"Debbie looked over her right shoulder and said, 'Mom, can you see him there standing in the corner?' I looked. We were alone in the room.

" 'No,' I replied honestly, 'I can't.'

"Debbie smiled. 'I didn't think you would be able to.'

"We talked some more. Then she looked me in the eye. She pointed past the foot of her bed toward the wall and asked, 'Can you see the door?'

" 'No,' I replied, 'I really can't see it.'

"Deb smiled. 'I thought you probably couldn't.'

"After more conversation, she held both of her hands about twelve inches in front of her face and asked if I could see the hazy, foggy curtain that was there. I knew what she was trying to communicate, so I said, 'Yes, I believe I can see what you are seeing.'

"She smiled a beautiful smile of joy, pleased that she had really communicated with me, and she was happy. Shortly after that, Deb's heart arrested.

"Who was the person that Deb had seen so clearly but was invisible to me? What was the unseen door? Where did it lead? I believe that Deb had seen her angel that had come to personally escort her through that doorway into the living, loving hands of Jesus. I will forever treasure that beautiful time of sharing although I will never be able to explain it fully."

Chapter 16

Do Angels Have a Sense of Humor?

"Angels can fly because they take themselves lightly," Gilbert Chesterton quipped.

Most people think of angels as always being serious. After all, aren't they God's servants, sent to do his divine bidding? When angels bring a message, it comes straight from God. The guardian angels intervene in life-and-death situations. Warrior angels frighten ordinary mortals and deter them from evil deeds. The seraphim spend all their time in worship before the heavenly throne of God. All this is serious business indeed.

Do angels have fun? Do they have a sense of humor? We don't find an answer to this question directly in the Bible, but there is reason to believe that at times angels do, indeed, take themselves lightly.

In the Bible angels think, exercise their will, and feel emotions. They have the characteristics of personality. We have no difficulty with thoughts of angels loving, comforting, and encouraging. It would follow that other characteristics of personality would also be a part of their makeup, including a sense of humor.

Seriousness of purpose and humor often go together. Members of small groups that study the Bible in earnest, share their deep needs, and pray fervently for one another, usually report that a kind of holy hilarity becomes a natural part of their meetings. Elton Trueblood in his book *The Humor of Christ* makes a very compelling case that Jesus had a fine sense of humor. As the creator of the angels it would be unlikely that Christ would make them humorless.

Angels do talk to each other. Can you imagine the conversation when one heavenly being shares with another his mission on earth? Could he keep a straight face when recounting the story of Baalam? Yes, it was grim business, confronting a prophet who was not above accepting a bribe. But how outrageously the angel acted to put the fear of the Lord in Baalam's heart! We read the story in Numbers 22. The prophet is riding his donkey when suddenly in the road the donkey sees an angel with a drawn sword pointed at her master's heart. If the donkey were to go ahead, Baalam would be run through by the angel's sword, so the donkey, in fear, runs off the road into the field. Now the Bible makes it clear that the donkey saw the angel but that the prophet did not, so the prophet beats the poor donkey until she goes back on the road.

Then they come to a narrow path between two vineyards, with walls on both sides. Again the angel appears, sword in hand. The frightened donkey presses close to the wall, crushing Baalam's foot against it. Again the prophet beats his donkey.

Then the angel moves on and stands in a narrow place where there was no place to turn, either to the left or right. When the donkey sees the angel with the sword, the animal lies down under Baalam. The prophet, in anger, beats the poor donkey.

The short story has a twist that outdoes O. Henry. Now the donkey talks. "Haven't I always been a good donkey? Have I made a habit of doing this to you? Then why do you beat me?"

What can top a talking donkey? The Lord opens Baalam's eyes, and he sees the angel with his drawn sword. The angel explains that if the donkey had gone ahead, the prophet would have been killed. Baalam is literally scared silly. He falls on his face in fear. As a result, instead of accepting a bribe and cursing the Israelites, Baalam braves the wrath of wicked King Balak and blesses Israel.

It is a great story of the importance of obedience to God and, along with its profound message, a very funny story. A funny, angel story.

Along with the serious stories people have told us, we have also heard others that struck us as being amusing as well, making us believe that angels do have a sense of humor. Here is one. Read it and decide for yourself if the angels themselves might have laughed at this unusual encounter.

Swing Low ...

It's the little foxes that spoil the grapes, the Old Testament writer reminds us. Little things can make our lives crazy. For Helen Shirling, it was a hammock.

At Christmas, Helen and her husband had always put their tree on their glassed-in front porch where it could be seen from the street as well as from the living room. To make room for the tree, they always moved the hammock from the porch to the basement.

Helen's husband had died the previous May, so this year he was not there to help. Taking the hammock apart had always been easy. With one person on each end, a quick tug was all that was needed to pull it apart. Tackling the job by herself was quite a different matter. Helen tried to push and pull at the same time, but the old hammock refused to budge. The grandchildren and the neighbor children had played hard on the hammock, and the frame seemed stuck for good.

Not really, Helen thought. *If I call my son, he would be glad to help me.* But Helen wanted to show that she could do for herself.

Helen tells the story: "I knew I should wait for my son to help me, but I wanted it done right now. You've heard the saying, 'Lord, grant me patience, but I want it right now.' We have a large basement, and when I couldn't budge the hammock, I thought I could just leave it together and drag it downstairs.

"I dragged the thing through the house, knocking things down as I went. When I got to the basement door, I found there was no way I could turn it around to go through the door and down the stairs. I was perspiring and disgusted with myself for not waiting for help that my son would have so willingly given me.

"I thought of Billy Graham's saying that we have personal angels. I cried out, 'If there are angels all around me, why don't they help me when I need it?'

"Right before my eyes that hammock fell apart. Pieces rolled across the floor and under the table. All I had to do was pick up the parts and carry them to the basement.

"I froze in my tracks when it happened. To this day I still get goose bumps when I tell about it.

"The family has never let me forget it, and they laugh about Helen's angels. Now whenever they see an angel figure in a store, they buy it for me."

For Helen, it's proof that angels help even when we don't deserve their assistance. She is still amazed that the angels were not so high-and-mighty that they weren't above taking a hammock apart.

Helen has a nice angel collection. "How did you get so many?" friends ask.

"It's a funny story," Helen replies.

Angelic Organization

Many people are fascinated with the ordering of angels and the naming of their ranks. Other Christians have never heard of the celestial hierarchy. How can it be that the organization of the angels is accepted as gospel by millions of Christians and remain unknown to millions of other Christians?

Before the Christian era, the Jews had a highly developed and elaborate system of angels. As the Christian church began, a group called Gnostics taught that there is a long series of intermediaries between man and God. One of the reasons that Paul wrote the epistle to the Colossians was to correct erroneous ideas that some held about angels. Biblical scholars refer to this as the Colossian heresy. In the first chapter of Colossians, Paul takes pains to assert the supremacy of Christ. Beginning with verse 15, Paul makes clear that Jesus is God, that he is the creator of everything including angels, and is over all things. Paul names four classes of angels included in the Colossian heresy: thrones, dominions, principalities, and powers (1:16 KJV). Paul repeats the theme in Ephesians 1:21 KJV), where he writes that Christ is "Far above all principality, and power, and might (or virtue), and dominion, and every name that is named."

An important book in the development of theology about angels is *The Celestial Hierarchy* by Dionysius the Areopagite. From the sixth century through the Middle Ages it was believed to have been written by the first-century Greek who was converted by Saint Paul at

Athens (Acts 17:34). It was treated as an authority almost equal to the Bible because it was thought that Paul had personally instructed Dionysius and taught him the special revelation about angels and the angelic order that the apostles Paul and John had received in visions. The speculative ideas in the book were generally accepted in the centuries that followed, especially after their endorsement by Pope Gregory the Great (A.D. 590–604).

In the thirteenth century Thomas Aquinas, in his book *Summa Theologica*, developed and explained the ideas in Dionysius's book. Aquinas gave the organization of the angels and used the words from the Scripture listed above, placing them in three choirs:

First Choir

1. Seraphim
2. Cherubim
3. Thrones

Second Choir

1. Dominions
2. Virtues
3. Powers

Third Choir

1. Principalities
2. Archangels
3. Angels

The first choir was the highest, and at the top were the seraphim, who were always in God's presence, engaged solely in worship. At the lower end of the order were the angels and archangels, whose duties included leading, guarding, and guiding humans.

Later it was discovered that *The Celestial Hierarchy* was not written by Dionysius and was not in existence until the sixth century. The Reformers, such as Luther and Calvin, rejected the notion of three choirs of angels, insisting that all we could know for certain is what was written in the Bible. Calvin wrote about Dionysius's book that the greatest part of it was mere babbling. Karl Barth dismissed Dionysius as "one of the greatest frauds in church history." Today he is referred to as Pseudo-Dionysius.

Generally, Protestants divide the angelic order only into angels and archangels. They take the other terms, such as principalities, dominions, and thrones, to describe functions that the angels perform.

The only angel specifically called an archangel in the Bible is Michael (Jude 9). According to Billy Graham, Michael must stand alone "because the Bible never speaks of archangels, only *the* archangel."* In the Old Testament, Michael is closely identified with the Jewish nation and called "Michael, the great prince who protects your people." In Revelation 12 Michael is the head of the heavenly host that defeats the Devil and his angels.

Although only Michael is specifically called an archangel in the Scripture, some theologians state that the argument from silence does not prove that he is the only one. In Daniel 10:13 an angel says, "Then Michael, one of the chief princes, came to help me." Is a chief prince in heaven the same as an archangel? That text seems to imply that Michael may be one of several archangels. The Catholic Church agrees and includes Gabriel as

*Billy Graham, *Angels, God's Secret Agents*, Word Books, 1986 edition, 48.

an archangel. Gabriel appears more prominently in both the Old and New Testaments than does Michael. He is remembered best for his appearance to Mary, telling her that she would be the mother of Jesus. According to Jewish legend, it was Gabriel who destroyed Sodom and Gomorrah.

The Catholic Church also acknowledges Raphael as an archangel. Raphael appears only in the book of Tobit as Tobiah's companion on the road to Nineveh. He refers to himself as one of the seven who stand before the throne of God. From that, some have suggested that Raphael is one of seven archangels.

There will always be differences of opinion about the angelic organization—until we get to heaven and discover firsthand what it is. Until then, there is one truth of which we may be certain. The angelic hierarchy is completely different from the bureaucracy we find here on earth. *There is no inefficiency, no needless duplication of effort, and no work left undone.* The angels work in perfect harmony in the service of God and as ministering spirits to mankind.

What Do Angels Look Like?

What comes to mind when you think of an angel? A towering blond figure with wings and flowing robes, protecting two children crossing a rickety bridge? A chubby Victorian cherub? Michael Landon in *Highway to Heaven*, or Delbert in the classic film *It's a Wonderful Life*? What do angels look like, according to those who have experienced them and the records in the Bible?

Usually angels are unseen. This is not surprising, because angels are spirit beings: minds without physical bodies. The Bible indicates that angels constantly carry out God's bidding in caring for people, yet most people are not aware of ever seeing an angel.

In Numbers 22 Baalam finds his donkey leaving the road. Baalam is puzzled until later when he learns that the maneuvers of the donkey were owing to an angel that he did not see. Today most of us don't ride donkeys, but if you bring up the subject of angels and automobiles many people will tell of what seemed to be a miraculous escape from an accident. Often no angel was seen, but they are convinced there is no other explanation for the events except that an angel was present and at work. Others have sensed an angelic presence without seeing a form. Many people, in looking back, become aware that what appeared to be coincidence at the time may have been the work of unseen angels.

When angels do appear, most often they take on familiar, human form in order to do their work without frightening us. The Bible does not explain how spirit beings can assume bodies. It simply teaches that they do and that we do not recognize them as angels because they look like ordinary people. The angels who appeared to Abraham and Lot in the book of Genesis looked like and were dressed as ordinary people. How often do angels come in human form? Probably more often than we realize. "Do not forget to entertain strangers," Hebrews 13:2 admonishes us, "for by so doing some people have entertained angels without knowing it." The passage suggests that at *any* time it is *possible* that we may have encountered angels without our being conscious of their supernatural nature.

One reason for this phenomenon is that when angels do appear, most often they come in a human form most characteristic of those living in that area. Abraham's angels dressed and looked like people of his day. In the accounts included in *A Rustle of Angels*, a missionary to the Andes saw an angel that looked like a national from Ecuador; a Mexican family saw two angels who looked like Mexicans; in Haiti the angels were very black; white Americans saw angels who resembled their neighbors; black persons saw black angels. This is to be expected. Being inconspicuous is often a part of the angel's ministry.

At times there are exceptions. The Good Samaritan-type angel sometimes appears as a person of another race or culture. God is good at breaking down walls of prejudice.

Some report seeing angels that are awesome. Many times God's hosts have appeared as warrior angels, tremendously tall and powerful. Others have seen angels as beautiful beings with wings. There may be times when a person's faith is bolstered if an angel appears in a more traditional form.

Others report the angelic presence as light. In Exodus

3:2 the angel of the Lord appears to Moses as flames in the burning bush. In Psalm 104:4 angels are a flaming fire. Many have told us that they have seen an angel appear as light. At times it begins as a faint glow that grows until the room is filled with brilliance. At other times it is as though there is a figure unseen, because it is bathed in light. Some are able to describe what the angel was wearing but could not see the features of his face because it was bathed in a bright light. Could this be where our idea of a halo originated? Many observers tell of a pure white light, brighter than any whiteness they have ever seen; others describe different colors. For several it was pink; others found it to be iridescent like mother-of-pearl; two described it as cobalt blue, while many said it was indescribable, completely different from anything they had ever seen.

Sometimes the form is seen, but the facial features are hidden in a heavenly aura. A number of people describe a ball of light that sometimes passes right through the wall of a building.

Many who have been present at the death of a loved one tell of a light that entered the room in the final moments of life, then gently rose as though escorting the unseen spirit of the dying person into the presence of God.

Angel-visited people have described the eyes of these spirits more than any other feature. They were struck by the depth of love and compassion in the angels' eyes, which left them with a deep sense of peace.

What do angels look like? Angels are unseen spirits. If it is helpful as they do their ministry, they may take on a form that we humans see. This is only a temporary accommodation—not what angels really look like but only the form in which an angel has chosen to appear temporarily.

After death, when we are given a spiritual body, will we see angels as spirits? No doubt. What will they look like? Completely different from anything our physical eyes have seen. The hints that the Bible gives us indicate that angels are awesome, glorious, and beautiful beyond description. "No eye has seen, no ear has heard, no mind has conceived what God has prepared for those who love him" (1 Cor. 2:9).

Chapter
19

How Can I Meet an Angel?

Wouldn't it be wonderful to see an angel? How does one do it?

Today there are books on how to talk with your guardian angel. In many places seminars are given on the subject. What does the Bible say about how you can see an angel?

Absolutely nothing! And this must be significant. If God wanted us to see our guardian angel, he surely would have given us the instructions in the Bible, the place we turn for guidance in spiritual matters. If God intended us to communicate with the angels, such important directions would have been included in the Scriptures.

The Bible does teach us how to communicate with God through a method that we call *prayer*. Jesus taught about prayer.

You will also find prayer to God taught in the Epistles but not how to talk to an angel. The omission is not accidental, because angels are not to take the place of God. When we have the need to talk to a supernatural being, God is the One whom we should address.

The times in the Bible that people encountered angels were never because of persons requesting such. It was not because they had practiced some religious exercises to open themselves to the presence of angels. In the Bible, it is always the angel's choice. People see an angel when the angel decides to be seen. Or, put more correctly, in the Bible, people see an angel when it is God's will for them to see an angel.

The clear teaching of the Bible also is that many times angels are with us but we do not recognize them because they look like ordinary people. It is possible that you have seen them but did not know it. It is possible that they have ministered to you and that you were unaware of their true identity.

We must accept the fact that it is up to God if and when we encounter an angel in our lives. As we have seen in the accounts given in this book, angels show up at the most unexpected times. Sometimes they appear at important times; sometimes they come for what we consider insignificant events.

But when we read the Bible there are some patterns. There are some times that angels did appear in the life of Christ. These are also times that an angel is likely to minister to you whether you are aware of him or not.

1. When We Are Heartbroken or Are Facing a Difficult Decision

In the Garden of Gethsemane Jesus prayed: "Take this cup from me; yet not my will, but yours be done." An angel "from heaven" came and ministered to him.

Even though we may not see them, we may be sure that God's angels are ministering to us especially in those difficult times when we are seeking his will.

2. When We Face Temptation

When Jesus was tempted, the angels came and ministered to him. When we face temptation, we may be sure that the angels are only a prayer away, ready to help.

We find it so easy to say, "The Devil made me do it."

If it is not difficult to believe that the Evil One gives tempting thoughts, why should it be hard to believe the good angels influence our thoughts and are helping us to stand up to temptation?

3. When We Are Doing God's Will

The life of Christ teaches us that we may always expect the angels to be near us when we are doing God's will. They may be unseen, but they are always there. It may be that sometime in this life we may have that glorious, faith-affirming experience of seeing an angel.

4. At the Time of Death

We do know that at the time of death they will bring us to heaven, where we will join the glorious heavenly hosts in the praise and worship of God.

Many people have reported seeing angels come at the time of death, and some of those accounts are included in this book. The belief that angels come for us when we die is not simply based on anecdotal evidence. It is found in the teachings of Jesus. In Luke 16:22 Jesus taught that when the beggar Lazarus died, the angels carried him to heaven. The angels did more than escort him; they carried him! Sometimes the angelic beings not only take the dying person to be home with the Lord, but they also bring comfort and hope to those who remain, sustaining them in their loss.

What a joy to know that we will see an angel—at least at the time of death!

We Are Not Angels in the Making

In the thousands of letters that people have written to us we have learned that there are many different ideas as to what angels are. It is easy to understand the confusion. Part of it arises from the fact that the word, *angel*, from the beginning could refer either to a human or a supernatural being. The Hebrew word for angel in the Old Testament and the Greek word in the New Testament meant *messenger*. Whether the "messenger" was human or heavenly had to be determined by the clues in the context.

It is the same in the English language. *Webster's Tenth New Collegiate Dictionary* includes the following definitions for *angel*: *(1) a spiritual being superior to man in power and intelligence; one in the lowest rank in the celestial hierarchy; (2) an attendant spirit or guardian; (3) a white-robed winged figure of human form in fine art. (4) MESSENGER, HARBINGER (of death); (5) a person like an angel; (6) inspiration from God; (7) one (as a backer of a theatrical venture) who aids or supports with money or influence.*

Most of the time we are clear in our use of the word. When someone does something helpful for us and we say, "You're an angel!" we do not expect that person to suppose that we regard him as a supernatural being. Other times, as in the anecdotes in this book, it is clear that those who have described an encounter with an angelic being were not speaking of a kind human being but of a "heavenly" angel.

Quite often, though, the lines of distinction are blurred. This is due partly to our popular culture. A common plot in television and motion pictures is the story of a person who dies and comes back as a guardian angel. The film classic, *It's a Wonderful Life* starring Jimmy Stewart, is a familiar example of this idea.

Do people really believe this? Yes! We received a lengthy letter from a Delbert (not his real name). He states: "Billy Graham's book on angels is not the way. Angels are departed Christians who want to help persons as they go through this life—usually a loved one or friend." Delbert believes that he has a special angel, Laura, who was in love with him from the second grade. Unfortunately Delbert did not know this, and when he married, poor Laura died of a broken heart. Now she has returned to be his guardian angel. This certainly must be comforting to Delbert. He did not mention what his wife thinks of the arrangement!

Delbert is not alone in his belief. Reinforced by stories in books and movies as well as the wish that many have for their dead loved one to be near them, this notion is held by many.

Gary Soulsman, writing an article that was carried in the Gannett chain of newspapers quotes a common opinion: "Angels are nothing more than human beings who have lived and died. We are all potentially angels with different qualities and characteristics. We are angels in the making."

Another popular idea is found in the touching Christmas story, *The Littlest Angel*. The book has been a bestseller for years and the television adaptation is repeated often during the Christmas season. It is the touching story of a little boy who died and became an angel. His most cherished possession, his toy box, becomes the star of Bethlehem.

Many people are comforted by the thought that their child who died has become an angel. As a pastor, Bill has often heard this idea expressed when he has conducted the funeral for a baby. According to the Bible, angels are *not* humans who have died, whether babies or adults. According to Colossians 1:16, angels are among the invisible beings created by God. Biblical theologians point out a difference between mediate and immediate creation. In the Genesis account, God created Adam, then made Eve from Adam's rib. The first parents had children, their children had children, and the process continues to this day. While God is the creator in the beginning, people now result from being born. The theologians call this "*mediate* creation."

In contrast, God created angels. Every angel has been directly created by God from nothing. Angels do not give birth to baby angels. The only way an angel has ever come into existence is to have been created by God. Every angel came into existence as the result of a direct command from God. Theologians call this "*immediate* creation."

People are *born*. Angels are *created*.

This is what Jesus referred to in Matthew 22:30 when he said, "At the resurrection people will neither marry nor be given in marriage; they will be like the angels in heaven."

Angels do not die. Once God has created an angel, the angel continues to exist. On earth, if people had not had children, within a generation everyone would have died and there would be no one on earth. It is not like that with angels. God did not make them able to reproduce, because there was no reason for them to do so. God has created every angel necessary, and they all continue to be, to this day.

The exact time of their creation is not known, but Job 38:7 tells us that they shouted with joy at the creation of the world.

At present we humans are lower than the angels. Psalm 8:4–5 states: "What is man that you are mindful of him, the son of man that you care for him? You made him a little lower than the heavenly beings."

The great news of the Gospel is that we will not *remain* a little lower than the angels. As explained in Hebrews 2:9–10: "Jesus . . . was made a little lower than the angels" when he came to earth, identified himself with the human race, and "suffered death, so that by the grace of God he might taste death for everyone." The verses following explain that when a person accepts the salvation that comes through faith in Jesus Christ he or she is brought into the family of God. "So Jesus is not ashamed to call them brothers" (v. 11).

What happens when Christians die? They go to heaven, not to be lower than the angels but to claim their inheritance of being "heirs of God and joint heirs with Christ." That's far better than being an angel. What a tremendous salvation! Although the angels, who are always wanting the best for us, rejoice when a person becomes a Christian (Luke 15:10), they do not comprehend the love of God that has made such provision for us. Peter writes about our salvation: "Even angels long to look into these things" (1 Peter 1:12).

And what about babies who die? They are safe in the arms of Jesus. The angels carry them to heaven. Hebrews 2:9 points out that Christ tasted death for everyone. These precious little ones are included in the Atonement. It is rejecting Christ that keeps one from heaven, and since babies have never done this they go from this life to life eternal because of the finished work of Christ. God has prepared something much better for babies who die than for them to become angels. They do not have to go through the trials and the problems of our earthly life. They do receive the gift of eternal life through Jesus Christ our Lord. Instead of remaining a baby, they will reach their full potential in heaven and have a glorious future, being placed far above the angels. What a comfort that is for anyone who has lost a child.

Chapter
21

Hell's Angels

At one glorious point in eternity past, God created the angels. Of the millions of the heavenly hosts, Lucifer, son of the morning, the light-bearer, was the most outstanding. In Ezekiel 28 we find this description:

> *You were the model of perfection,*
> *full of wisdom and perfect in beauty.*
> *You were in Eden, the garden of God; . . .*
> *You were anointed as a guardian cherub . . .*
> *You were blameless in your ways*
> *from the day you were created*
> *till wickedness was found in you.*
>
> (vv. 12–15)

God created Lucifer; and he saw that all he created was good. But Lucifer of his own choice sinned against God. Ezekiel explains it simply:

> *Your heart became proud*
> *on account of your beauty*
> *and you corrupted your wisdom*
> *because of your splendor.*
>
> (v. 17)

In a parallel passage of dual reference, Isaiah describes the sins that led to the fall of Lucifer:

> *You said in your heart,*
> *"I will ascend to heaven;*
> *I will raise my throne*

> *above the stars of God;*
> *I will sit enthroned on the mount of assembly,*
> *on the utmost heights of the sacred mountain.*
> *I will ascend above the tops of the clouds;*
> *I will make myself like the Most High."*
> *(Isaiah 14:13–14)*

The created being, Lucifer, because of his pride and desire to be like God himself, influenced other angels to follow in his path of sin. Many Bible scholars believe as many as one third of the angels fell with Lucifer (Rev. 12:4). God expelled them from heaven. Lucifer became known as Satan, which means *the accuser.*

The Bible does not give a systematic account of Satan. We find references to the Devil and to the evil angels and their work, throughout the Bible. To understand it, we try to put together the pieces. Our problems in being dogmatic are:

1. Many of the Scriptures that speak about Satan are poetical or apocalyptical, as in the book of Revelation. In other words, many of the references are figurative. For example, in Revelation 12 the Devil is pictured as a dragon.

2. Many of the biblical references are in passages talking about another subject. In Ezekiel 28 judgment is pronounced against the king of Tyre. But the prophecy has a dual reference, referring to the judgment of Lucifer as well.

Here are some things we do learn:

1. Satan and his angels are minds without bodies; that is, like angels, they are spirits. The description of Satan in the Scripture indicates that he was the brightest and most intelligent of the angels.

2. Satan and his angels, like all angels, were created by God before the creation of the world. When our world was made, "all the angels shouted for joy" (Job 38:7).

3. They were not created as evil in essence. God would not—yes, could not—create evil. They were created as good in essence, and they fell of their own choice.

4. When did this happen? *After* the Creation—for "God saw all that he had made, and it was very good" (Genesis 1:31). But it was *before* the temptation in the Garden of Eden.

5. How? Paul calls it the "mystery of iniquity" (2 Thess. 2:7 KJV), or "the secret power of lawlessness" (2 Thess. 2:7 NIV). Mortimer J. Adler says that it is extremely difficult to understand. "In the inscrutability of Satan's choice lies the mystery of evil."

It was pride, Lucifer's love of self, that made Lucifer reject the gift of grace. Loving himself more than he loved God, he wished to attain *without* God's grace that which is only attainable *through* it.

6. Lucifer's sin led to judgment. Rev. 12:7–9: "There was war in heaven. Michael and his angels fought against the dragon, and the dragon and his angels fought back. . . . The great dragon was hurled down—that ancient serpent called the devil, or Satan, who leads the whole world astray. He was hurled to the earth, and his angels with him."

7. There is no doubt about the final outcome. God will prevail. Satan and his angels will ultimately be totally defeated. They will be eternally punished and unable to frustrate believers or interfere with God's will.

Let's not delve too far into the physical descriptions of hell. The angels do not have physical bodies. They do not feel pain as in the heat of hell.

The theologian, Thomas Aquinas wrote: "The devils do feel something that corresponds to the physical pain, only worse. Namely the frustrations of their will, the darkening of their intellect."

Such words as *light*, *darkness*, and *presence* must be

shorn of their physical connotations to understand what the Bible is saying. The holy angels are in the realm of light in the presence of God. The evil angels are in darkness and are devoid of light and isolated from the presence of God.

8. The primary activity of Satan today is to tempt humans. He does this primarily by being the deceiver, the liar. Most often, it is not by asking a person to do raw evil. Rather it is by suggesting that good can come from doing things that are not God's will. He suggests, "I don't mean to hurt anyone, only help them," but the actions that he suggests are not God's ways.

9. We are not powerless when we are tempted. God provides the help of his grace and the good angels. People find it easy to believe that "the Devil made me do it." The Bible teaches that the good angels are also present, working to help us resist temptation and to make the right choices. Charles Wesley wrote:

> *Angels, where'er we go,*
> *Attend our steps whate'er betide.*
> *With watchful care their charge defend,*
> *And evil turn aside.*

10. God sets limits on what Satan and the evil angels can do. This is made clear in the book of Job. First Corinthians 10:13 makes it clear that God controls Satan's attacks on believers.

Discernment

Life is not easy. Making choices can be tough. For the Christian, the Holy Spirit leads and guides, but the Devil also seeks to influence each person. What complicates the decision-making process is that Satan often disguises himself as an angel of light.

In his grace, God sends his holy angels to light, guard, and guide. The evil angels are also at work trying to influence each person as well.

We humans are caught in the crossfire of their struggle. Is there hope? Yes! Can we separate the true from the false? With God's help, yes!

Take courage, for although there is a spiritual struggle, good and evil are not evenly matched. God is the Creator; Satan is a created being. God is all-powerful; the Devil's power is limited. God knows all things. While Satan knows more than humans comprehend, he does not know as much as God knows. God is everywhere at all times; the leader of the fallen angels can only be in one place at a time. *God is not limited in any way.* Satan can only act within the boundaries God has set. He is, after all, in Luther's startling phrase, "God's Devil," always on a chain, albeit a long one. It is to be remembered that "God . . . will not let you be tempted beyond what you can bear" (1 Corinthians 10:13). The holy angels far outnumber the evil angels.

Satan will not be able to thwart God's plan. God will triumph, and Satan will be defeated.

Given this spiritual warfare, what are the survival

techniques? How can a person tell what is of God and what is from the Evil One? The Bible calls this the gift of *discernment.*

Point of discernment one: God and the holy angels will never tell you anything that is contrary to what is found in the Bible. God's message will always agree with the clear teachings of Scripture.

John had been hurt by Erick. John did not deserve the hurt. It went deep—deep enough to lodge itself securely in his memory. It hurt, and it kept on hurting.

One night as John slept, he had a very vivid dream of an angel who spoke to him, instructing: "Don't forgive. Get even." In the dream a plan unfolded, a clever plan that John had never thought of. It was a way to get even with Erick without anyone's knowing that John was behind it. And Erick would be hurt far more deeply than John had been.

John awoke. The angel in the dream was unforgettable and the message so clear. John was a Christian, so he asked himself, "Was this a message from God?" He decided to test it from the Scripture. That morning he read from 2 Corinthians 2: "You ought to forgive . . . in order that Satan might not outwit us. For we are not unaware of his schemes."

This was not a new idea to John. Throughout the Bible the importance of forgiveness is stressed. He realized that it could not have been one of God's holy angels speaking to him in a dream because the message was not in keeping with the teachings of Scripture.

Point of discernment two: A message from God's angels will always be in the spirit of Christ. We can find the spirit of Christ as we meditate on his life and teachings. John asked, "What would Jesus do? Would he get even?" Immediately he knew the answer. Jesus taught that we are to forgive seventy times seven times—and Erick had hurt him only once. On the cross Jesus prayed, "Father, forgive them." John was hurting, but his pain could not be compared with what Jesus suffered. To act in the spirit of Christ would mean to forgive. The message, "Don't forgive. Get even," could not have come from God. It could have come from the subconscious mind, which often influences our dreams. John acknowledged that he did want to strike back and wound Erick more than he himself had been hurt. The message may have come from one of Satan's angels. Perhaps the vividness of the dream could be an indication of the Evil One at work.

Point of discernment three: A genuine encounter with an angel will always glorify God, not the angel. Angels do not draw attention to themselves. Billy Graham writes, "It is no accident that angels are usually invisible." Most often when they do appear, they resemble ordinary people, but it is true that sometimes people have seen the exquisite beauty and awesome power of angels. At the resurrection of Jesus, Matthew describes the angel: "His appearance was like lightning, and his clothes were white as snow. The guards were so afraid of him that they shook and became like dead men" (Matthew 28:3–4). The power of the angels pointed to the almighty God.

The angels themselves make it clear that attention, and especially worship, is to be directed to God alone. In the book of Revelation John writes, "I fell down to worship at the feet of the angel. . . . But he said to me, 'Do not do it! I am a fellow servant with you and of all who keep the words of this book. Worship God!'" (Revelation 22:8–9).

Angels typically do their work, then disappear. They don't wait to be thanked. Their purpose is to direct thanks to God. Landrum Leavell points out that "The faithful service of angels to mankind is not based on their love for you and me. It's based on their love for God." They act from love for God and to encourage us to love God more completely.

A common misconception is, "If you feel peace and contentment as a result of your experience, then you may be certain it was a valid angel experience." This is an oversimplification. The Devil and his angels, appearing like angels of light, are not above promising what seems to be good and attractive.

God's angels and their messages may sometimes be frightening, especially when they come to announce judgment. Think of the angels who came to visit Lot in Sodom. When the firstborn of the Egyptians were visited by the angel of death, grief and weeping resulted.

John Hicks was wasting his life by gambling, drinking, and doing drugs, when he saw an angel. He had never seen such anger as he saw in the eyes of the angel. It seemed that the being was filled with rage at the way John was wasting his life. John left the encounter frightened: scared straight. As a result of this terrifying ordeal, John found forgiveness through Christ and a new life. Noting these exceptions, we could state:

Point of discernment four: Angels ordinarily leave a person with an unexplainable sense of peace and a greater love for God. Those who have talked to us tell us that this is not fleeting. The sense of peace, comfort, and love remains, sometimes for a lifetime.

Point of discernment five: God's angels do not act to grant one person's selfish desires to the detriment of others. David Neff, managing editor of *Christianity Today*, wrote: "The angels of popular culture are more like celestial versions of the fairy godmother from Disney's Cinderella. . . . The angels of the tabloids are cosmic mascots who use magical powers to make our lives just a little sweeter than they might have been." Such concepts trivialize the work of angels. They are God's messengers. They come into our lives to do God's will. God's will is not to grant us three wishes, but that we do his will on earth as it is done in heaven. God's purpose is not to make life easy for us; it is to make us more Christlike. It is true that sometimes angels do small serendipitous acts of kindness but never in a way that hurts others.

Point of discernment six: Prayer should be used to confirm the genuineness of an encounter with an angel. As we pray to God the Father, the Holy Spirit will lead us into truth. God in his grace sends angels to minister to us. Because Satan and the evil angels are also a reality, we need to test the spirits. When in doubt, claim the promise of James 1:5: "If any of you lacks wisdom, he should ask God, who gives generously to all without finding fault, and it will be given to him."

Chapter
23

Be Like an Angel!

In *A Rustle of Angels* we have seen that the Bible teaches that we are for a little while a little lower than the angels. We are to worship only the Creator, God himself, not angels. Even the angels make this clear. They will not be worshiped but instead say, "Worship God!" (Revelation 22:9).

What should our attitude be toward angels? Certainly we should wonder at their beauty, marvel at their strength, and admire their holiness. We should be very appreciative of their work. "Are not all angels ministering spirits sent to serve those who will inherit salvation?" (Hebrews 1:14).

In teaching us about angels in the Bible, God has also given us a great example to follow. We, too, should make it our aim to please God. We should be obedient to God in all things, just as his holy angels are. Although we may not reach the goal of loving God with all our hearts as the angels do, that should be our aspiration while we are on this earth. The angels have already been confirmed in holiness. That, too, should be our goal, although this will be completed only when we enter the presence of Jesus Christ.

There are many ways that angels set the example for us to consider.

Be Like an Angel! Look for Ways to Serve God.

Betty Malz, in *Angels Watching Over Me*, writes that in the Bible and today, all the people whom angels assisted seemed to be caught in some kind of gap in which they had a need that they were powerless to meet. At these times God sent his angels.

This was the authors' experience when angels intervened in our lives.

It may be that often angels are God's second choice as intervenors. People can do many of the things that angels do. We believe that there are times when a person needs help, encouragement, support, or direction. God's first choice may often be to use a Christian. Perhaps if we as humans are unable or unwilling to meet the need, then God sends his angels.

Be Like an Angel,
Be There When God Needs You!

Of course there are things that angels can do that people cannot do. The Bible teaches, for example, that angels are not all-powerful although they are superior in strength to humans.

Given that the word *angel* means "messenger," we would expect angels to set the example for us in giving God's message. They do this in several ways.

Like an Angel, Tell the Good News!

God used an angel to tell Mary of the birth of Jesus; angels announced to the shepherds in the fields the good news of his coming. Angels told the good news of Easter for the first time—"He is not here; he has risen!"

We, too, can tell the Good News of salvation. Indeed, we can do it better than the angels can, because we have experienced God's salvation firsthand. First Peter 1:12 tells us that the angels wonder about our great salvation.

In the Bible God often sent angels to tell what would

happen, as in the birth of Jesus. You remember that the angel warned Mary and Joseph to flee because Herod would seek to kill the baby Jesus. In Acts 27 the angel told Paul that he would not be drowned at sea but would bring the message of God to Rome.

God didn't give his message this way very often in biblical times. It was reserved for special occasions. It seems that is true today as well.

Can we be like the angels and tell the future?—not in the sense of being fortune-tellers. But in the Bible God has revealed the blessed hope that Christ will return. We can and should be telling this message.

When Jesus ascended into heaven, two angels gave the message that Jesus would come again (Acts 1:10–11). Be like the angels and tell the Good News that Jesus is coming again.

Angels Give Directions

In the Scripture, God used angels to give directions, to tell people what to do. God expects us humans to give directions, too. How do we know what God's directions are? Almost unfailingly, they are found in the Bible. God's Word makes it clear what message we are to share with others.

When we share God's message as we find it in the Bible, we are to do it confidently. Remember that we, too, are angels—in the sense that we are God's messengers, ambassadors for Christ.

Let's not be angels who have lost their voices!

Be like an angel. Confidently share the truths of the Bible. Today the world needs to learn about God's values, God's morals, and God's laws.

Be Like an Angel,
Help and Protect Those in Need.

Of course we have taught our two little grandchildren about angels! When we were visiting them at Christmas, the two girls got moved from their regular beds to make room for the additional family members. When Marilynn came in to waken them in the morning, she found that three-year-old Angela had fallen out of bed during the night and was sound asleep on the floor. Marilynn said, "Perhaps Angela's guardian angel caught her when she fell so that she didn't hurt herself and cry out." Her five-year-old sister, Aubrey, had a different idea of the ministry of guardian angels. "Maybe," Aubrey said, "her guardian angel put her hand over her mouth so she wouldn't wake me up when she cried!"

We're not sure that a guardian angel did either that December night. But we are certain that we do have guardian angels who do perform important ministries for believers and set the example that we are to help others in time of need.

We are to be God's human ministering angels. That means we are to help those in need.

Tony Campolo is fond of saying that if you want to meet Jesus today, go to where there is a need. In his own colorful way, Tony points out that Jesus always hung out with the poor and needy and still does today.

Although that's not our way of saying it, we know that the Bible clearly teaches that every Christian is to be concerned with those in need and being of help where possible.

Often the need is to help people in ways that are far from dramatic. For example, we love meeting our friends at church, but we need to be aware of that shy woman, the insecure girl, the person who doesn't feel that he fits in. How difficult life can be for them if no one rescues them.

In the movie *Home Alone*, the young boy is accidentally left at home when his family goes on vacation, and he blames himself for his family's disappearance. Feeling bad, he goes into a church. He confides to an old man sitting near him: "I don't know what I'm doing here. I feel like I don't belong anywhere."

The man replies, "The church is the right place to go when you don't feel that you belong."

That's right! But God expects us Christians to be ministering angels to those who feel that they don't belong.

Be like an angel. Help the poor, the powerless, the needy, and those who feel that they do not fit in.

Be Like an Angel, Worship God

In the Scriptures we find that a major activity of the angels is worship. Do not miss the importance of this. Dr. A. W. Tozer referred to worship as the forgotten jewel of the church. Not so in the Bible.

The angels are aware of the greatness and majesty of God and sing "Holy, Holy, Holy!" The Scriptures report that they worship the Lord at all times.

What a joy it will be when we get to heaven and join in that worship.

We can do nothing more important in life. And isn't it wonderful to know that as we worship, even now, the angels are joining us as we bring our praises?

The liturgical churches recognize this. As a regular part of their liturgy in each service the minister says, "And now with the angels, the archangels, and the hosts of heaven, we join in singing, 'Holy, holy, holy.' Be like an angel, rejoice!"

Too, let's not miss the example the angels set for us in Luke 15:10: "There is rejoicing in the presence of the angels of God over one sinner who repents."

What happens in your church when someone decides to accept Christ? Is it politely noticed? Let's, like the angels, make it a priority to rejoice at someone's becoming a Christian and be sure to share our joy with them.

Let's follow the example of the angels in serving God with loving obedience.

Chapter
24

Angelology: A Summary

Angelology, the study of angels, includes material found in the earlier chapters of the book, put together in a more systematic way to help the serious student. To this we have added the information necessary for a more complete doctrine of angels.

All About Angels?

It would be fantastic if we could write everything about angels. Thomas Aquinas, known as the "Angelic Doctor," attempted to do this in A.D. 1215. It was a time when tremendous crowds turned out to hear great teachers. People were very interested in the subject of angels, and in fifteen lectures given in the course of one week, Aquinas attempted to tell everything that was known about them. He also answered questions from the audience. His lectures were written down and became the basis for his treatment in his great work, *Summa Theologica*, the most brilliant piece of speculation on the subject of angels ever written. Aquinas drew upon Scripture and tradition, but because the sacred Scriptures do not answer many questions about angels, he added his own conjectures. The modern reader recognizes that many of his answers were based on the culture and tradition of his time.

This summary recognizes that many facts about angels are not known. The sacred Scriptures tell us what we need to know about angels but leave many questions unanswered. Where no definitive answers are given, we will refrain from speculation.

We humans have limitations in understanding supernatural or heavenly beings. No scientist will ever win a Nobel Prize for research in the sphere of angels. Spirits cannot be weighed or measured. Litmus paper or other tools of science are not applicable in the study of these celestial beings. The scientific method applies to earthly things but does not relate to the immaterial.

Where can we find information about angels? First, from the experiences people have had with angels. But since angels are the secret agents of both God and the Devil, we must be careful as we make deductions based solely on our observations and experiences.

The most reliable source of information on angels is God's revelation found in the Bible, which is filled with references to angels.

Where Does the Word Angel Come From?

In the Old Testament the Hebrew word for angel is *mal'akh*. In the New Testament the Greek word is *aggelos*. Both words mean *messenger*, one of the most frequent duties assigned to angels.

The word *angel* is applied in Scripture to an order of supernatural or heavenly beings whose business it is to act as God's messengers to men and as agents who carry out his will.

How Many Times Are Angels Mentioned in the Bible?

The word *angel* appears 292 times in thirty-five books of the Bible, but other words are also used to designate angels. In the *New International Version*, words for angels include *cherubim, seraphs, ministering spirits, watchers, sons of God, chariots of God, holy ones, morning stars, thrones, powers, rulers, authorities, heavenly bodies, and miracles.* Many biblical scholars would also include the four living creatures and the twenty-four elders in Revelation 4:6–10.

Because the term for angel is the ordinary word used for any messenger, it is only when one reads the word in context that we know if it refers to a human messenger or an angel of God. Sometimes it is impossible to tell which is meant, so it is not possible to have an exact count of the number of references to angels in the Bible. One thing is certain: Every time you open the Bible, there's a rustle of angels.

Where Did Angels Come From?

Every angel was created by God. Colossians 1:16 clearly states that Jesus Christ is the creator of angels (referred to here as *things invisible, thrones, powers, rulers and authorities*). This creator, Jesus, "is before all things, and in him all things hold together" (Colossians 1:17). As Billy Graham wrote, "Even the angels would cease to exist if Jesus, who is Almighty God, did not sustain them by his power."

There is a great difference between the creation of humankind and angels. According to the Bible, God created Adam, then made Eve, and from this first couple the rest of humankind were brought into existence by the natural means of birth. People are born; angels are created directly by God. Psalm 148 states, "Praise him, all his angels ... for he commanded and they were created."

Angels are a company; people are a race.

When Were the Angels Created?

The theologian Lewis Sperry Chafer gives the commonly accepted opinion that "It may be assumed according to Colossians 1:16 that angels were created simultaneously." In the beginning there was God. Then God created the angels. They were present at Creation, for the Lord in Job 38:7 says that when the world was created, "the morning stars sang together, and all the angels shouted for joy."

How Many Angels Are There?

More than we can count. The apostle John reported seeing ten-thousand-times-ten-thousand angels encircling the throne of God. That would be one hundred million in one place if we take the count literally. Most likely references, such as Hebrews 12:22, "to thousands upon thousands of angels in joyful assembly" indicate that the number of angels is beyond counting.

Are Angels Masculine Or Feminine?

Neither! "Angels are apparently without sex," writes theologian C. Fred Dickason. "We say 'apparently' because we are limited to human concepts of sex and its power." Jesus, in Matthew 22:28–30 clearly states that angels do not procreate nor marry. So they are without sex in the normal sense of the word. It could be that the celestial spirit beings have gender in ways that we do not know. C. S. Lewis presents his speculation about angelic genders in fictional form in the second volume of his space trilogy, *Perelandra.*

Only three angels are mentioned by name in the Bible. They are Michael, Gabriel, and the fallen angel, Lucifer. All are masculine names, as are the names of the angels found in the Apocrypha. But since the angels are a numberless multitude, no conclusion can be drawn from this small sampling.

Did Jesus Christ Ever Appear in the Form of an Angel?

Most students of the Bible would answer, "Yes." There is general agreement that "The Angel of the LORD" in the Old Testament is a theophany, or a visible appearance of Christ to humans.

At times in the Bible, angels are clearly angels. Other times the angel is identified with God. This is the case with the Old Testament use of "the angel of the LORD." Many believe the angel of the LORD was none other than Jesus Christ, coming to earth in a visible form before the Incarnation. Here is some evidence to support that view.

In the Bible there are times when the angel of the LORD turns out to be none other than God himself. When Hagar ran away from Sarah, the angel of the LORD found her. The angel of the LORD promised to do himself what only God can do (Genesis 16:10–12). The account continues in verse 13, "She gave this name to the LORD who spoke to her: 'You are the God who sees me.'" The "angel of the LORD" and the "LORD" (Yaweh or Jehovah) are clearly one and the same.

When this angel appeared to Moses in the well-known account of the burning bush (Exodus 3:2), it says, "The angel of the LORD appeared to him in flames of fire from within a bush."

Two verses later it says, "God called to him from within the bush." Here and other places in the Old Testament the words for God and the angel of the LORD are used interchangeably.

Yet the angel of the LORD is separate from God. In Zechariah (and elsewhere) the angel of the LORD talks to the LORD Almighty. How can the angel of the LORD be God and be separate from God at the same time? This mystery can be understood if we recognize it as being similar to Christ in his earthly life: being truly God yet being separate from God. So we find Jesus praying to the Father, as in John 17.

It is possible the angel of the LORD was simply an angel with a special commission. There seem to be fewer difficulties in understanding the ministry of the angel of the LORD if we see him as a momentary revelation of God on this earth.

When we read in the Bible the many references to the angel of the LORD, we ask, "Was it an angel? Or was it God?" There are times today when we are aware of divine intervention in our lives that we ask the same question.

Do Angels Die?

No! Jesus clearly taught in Luke 20:36 that once created, angels never die.

Do Angels Know Everything?

No! Angels have superhuman knowledge. They know more than people, but only God is omniscient. Informed by God, they do know some future events (Luke 1:13–16) and God's plan for the world (Revelation 17–18). At least at times they know the motives and purposes of people without being told (Matthew 28:5). We can be certain that God's holy angels use their knowledge for our good.

There are some things they do not know. Although they will be an important part of the events at the Second Coming of Christ, they do not know the day or hour when it will occur (Matthew 24:36). There are also some things they do not fully understand, including the sufferings of Christ and our great salvation. "Even angels long to look into these things" (1 Peter 1:12).

Do Angels Have Emotions?

Yes! They sang for joy at the creation of the world (Job 38:7). They rejoice when one sinner repents (Luke 15:10). They express awe and reverence in their worship of God. Even as their intelligence is greater than humans, so we may also suppose their ability to have deep and sensitive emotions is greater.

How Strong Are Angels?

They have tremendous strength! They are stronger and more powerful than men (2 Peter 2:11). In fact, according to theologian Landrum Leavell, "power, rather than beauty or even intelligence is their outstanding mark. They're better known for their power than anything else." In Scripture they are called "the mighty ones" and God's "powerful angels."

One angel is able to destroy the entire Assyrian army or completely wipe out Sodom and Gomorrah. But they are not all-powerful. Only God is omnipotent. There are things God can do that angels cannot. Only God can create. Angels sometimes require assistance from the Lord in their conflict with evil (Jude 9).

Where Do Angels Live?

The Bible repeatedly uses the phrase *the angels in heaven.* Heaven may be considered as home for the angels, but the answer may not be quite that simple. There is a difference of opinion about the heaven where the holy angels live.

Some say all angels live in heaven, which is the dwelling place of God. Some angels never leave these courts of heaven. Apparently the seraphs spend their time continuously in worship before the throne of God (Isaiah 6:1–6). In Luke 1:19 Gabriel identifies himself as one who stands in the presence of God.

Others say that angels live in the second heaven. According to 2 Corinthians 12:2 there are three heavens. These are usually understood to be: (1) the earth's atmosphere, (2) the heavens of the stars and planets, and (3) the presence of God. In this view, it is pointed out that Jesus, when he ascended, passed through the heavens (plural) into God's presence (Hebrews 4:14). Jesus is seated above all angelic principalities and powers (Ephesians 3:10), thereby implying that the angels are not in the first heaven but in the second. The angels would have access to the presence of God in the third heaven. This could be the picture of Job 1:6: "One day the angels came to present themselves before the Lord . . ."

Whether the abode of angels (to use the theologian's term) is the second or third heaven, it is clear that all angels do not stay in what we earthlings would call their primary residence. A guardian angel, for example, would be present on earth with the person in his charge.

What Do Angels Do in Heaven?

They Worship God. In Revelation 4 we catch a glimpse of the ceaseless worship of God by the angels. "Day and night they never stop saying, 'Holy, holy, holy is the Lord God Almighty, who was, and is, and is to come.'" Because of God's infinite worthiness, the worship of angels never ceases. "'You are worthy, our Lord and God, to receive glory and honor and power, for you created all things, and by your will they were created and have their being'" (Revelation 4:11).

It is easy for humans to underestimate the importance of worship. In the divine scheme of things it is the most important activity. Too often on earth, worship is what Robert Webber calls "the forgotten jewel." A part of our problem is that we are more attuned to the physical than to the spiritual. This will change when the believers enter heaven, and putting away earthly things, enter the manifest presence of God. Then we will be able to join the angels in the pure worship of God. Nothing can compare with that. Nothing is more important than that.

Angels Administer God's Government. Passages such as Psalm 103:19–22 point out that as God rules over all creation, he uses his angels to do his will and carry out his bidding. This includes much more than our world. It would encompass the entire universe and any other universes that God may have created.

The angels are also active behind the scenes in controlling the affairs of nations. Daniel 10 gives us a glimpse into their activity. The evil angels are also busy influencing the course of the nations, and God's holy angels continually oppose them.

Angels Rejoice When a Sinner Repents. There is joy in the presence of the angels of God over every sinner who repents (Luke 15:10).

What Do the Angels Do on Earth?

The greater part of this book explains and gives examples of the ministry of angels in this world. These are activities angels performed in biblical times. It is important to note that angels are very active today in the same types of service. Here is a brief summary presented in outline form. A more complete discussion is found in the chapters on each subject.

They Serve As Guardian Angels. This is the first function that comes to mind for most people. Angels carry out God's will by protecting and delivering their charges from harm.

The Warrior Angels Do Battle for God. These powerful angels are victorious against human armies. They also may do battle for a single individual. Sometimes the mere sight of a warrior angel is enough to frighten people and deter them from their intended evil acts. Warrior angels also do battle with the evil angels, and will ultimately defeat the Devil and his angels.

Angels Carry Out God's Justice. In Scripture we read that tens of thousands of angels were at Mount Sinai at the giving of the Law. In the New Testament it is stated that the Law was put into effect through angels (Acts 7:53. See also Galatians 3:19 and Hebrews 2:2). In the Exodus, God provided an angel to lead the Israelites out of Egypt. God warned them, "Pay attention to him, and listen to what he says. Do not rebel against him; he will not forgive your rebellion, since my Name is in him" (23:20–21). Here the angel stands clearly for God's law, order, and justice. Angels mete out punishment, as in the destruction of Sodom.

Angels Give Encouragement. They come at difficult times to rescue people from discouragement. At times the words they speak bring comfort and cheer. At other times the presence of an angel is enough to assure a person of God's love and care. Or they may tell the positive outcome of a situation. In Acts 27:23–24 Paul was told by an angel that he would be saved from death at sea so that he could minister to Rome.

Angels Strengthen People. They come to help a person through a time of pain, suffering, or hardship. In this role they do not rescue a person from an ordeal. They do help an individual to face whatever may come. The angel who ministered to Jesus in the Garden of Gethsemane is an example. This did not keep Jesus from the suffering of the cross, but this ministry strengthened him to endure it.

Angels Are Messengers. The word *angel* means "messenger." This is the major ministry that angels perform for God. In the Bible, God frequently used his angels as messengers. This is illustrated in the Christmas story. Angels told Mary that she was to be the mother of Jesus, explained the coming birth to Joseph, announced the Nativity to the shepherds, and told Joseph to flee to Egypt.

Angels Help People Realize That They Have Been Cleansed from Sin. The classic example is in Isaiah 6:6–7: A seraph with a live coal in his hand, which he had taken with tongs from the altar, flew to Isaiah. Touching Isaiah's mouth he said, "See, this has touched your lips; your guilt is taken away and your sin atoned for."

Angels Guide and Direct the Thoughts of People. Satan and the evil angels use their power to tempt people to sin. God's holy angels are also active, helping us to resist temptation. God also uses his angels to guide and direct in daily activities. Sometimes an angel appears; other times an angel speaks without being seen. Angels may influence our thoughts without our being aware of their ministry. This is also the work of the Holy Spirit in the life of a believer. The Bible does not tell us how to know if such guidance comes from the Holy Spirit or from an angel. In reality, it does not matter how God chooses to work, for the results would be similar and the glory would always go to God. Some suggest that God used the angels to guide and direct more frequently before the coming of the Holy Spirit at Pentecost. The ministry of angels is primarily external and physical. The ministry of the Holy Spirit is internal and spiritual.

Angels Help Bring a Person to Salvation. An angel directed Philip to go to the wilderness where he met the Ethiopian eunuch and led him to Christ (Acts 8:26). Another directed Cornelius to Peter who would tell him how to be saved (Acts 10:1–8). We may infer that angels are also influencing people today toward faith in God even when an audible voice is not heard. There is joy in the presence of angels when a sinner repents.

Angels Are Watchers. "A watcher, a holy one," is the description of the angel in Daniel 4:13 KJV. Angels are spectators, watching as we live out our lives. Paul says we are a "spectacle" to them (1 Corinthians 4:9). "Our certainty that angels right now witness how we are walking through life should mightily influence the decisions we make. God is watching, and his angels are interested spectators, too," says Billy Graham. What an incentive this should be to us to live consistent Christian lives!

Angels at the Time of Death. Jesus taught that at death the angels carry a person to heaven (Luke 16:22). What a wonderful, comforting thought! So many have given witness to the presence of angels at the time of death. Many times people present with the dying person have also seen the angels.

Why Don't Guardian Angels Always Save Us?

It's not because there are not enough guardian angels to go around, or that angels sometime take vacations. The angels always do God's will, so the real question is, "Why does God allow bad things to happen to good people?" This subject would require a complete book to suggest satisfactory answers. For a brief explanation, see our chapter, "But Where Was My Guardian Angel?"

Do Angels Only Help Good Christian People?

Angels do help good Christians. In fact, that is one of their primary missions. Hebrews 1:14 says all angels are "ministering spirits sent to serve those who will inherit salvation."

A question that perplexes many is, "Why do bad things happen to good people?" Some are even more disturbed by the question, "Why do good things happen to bad people?"

Angels do help people who are not of the household of faith. The first time the word *angel* is used in the Bible, the angel appears to an Egyptian maidservant, Hagar (Genesis 16). Sarah must have thought it was unfair of God to send an angel to the troublemaker she hated most. It wasn't until years later, and after the angel had rescued Hagar and Ishmael from death, that three angels would come to Abraham and Sarah with the news that they would have a child of their own.

In the New Testament, a Roman centurion, before he became a Christian, had an experience with an angel (Acts 10:17). We have heard several people who were not "good Christians" relate their experiences when angels came to their aid.

Why does God have angels help unbelievers? That is God's business. God is free to do what he desires. God is merciful and noted for his lovingkindness. He makes the rain to fall on the just and on the unjust alike. God is like that! Apparently he provides guardian angels for every person.

In the biblical account of Cornelius, the result of the experience with the angel was that the centurion did come to saving faith. That was also the result for several people whose accounts are in this book. It is possible that in every case it is the loving purpose of God that the intervention of angels will lead to belief in the God of the angels. Some, however, do not respond to him, no matter what way the Gospel comes to them.

Are Angels a Part of the New Age Movement?

Some within the New Age spirituality completely ignore angels. Other groups in the New Age overemphasize angels. Some New Age ideas are contrary to the Bible and traditional Christianity. These include channeling, angels as spirit guides, reincarnation—with people sometimes evolving into angels—and communing with your angel.

Unfortunately, because of the misuse of angels by the New Age movement, some people consider all teachings on angels to be suspect. We need to keep a balance and test all teachings and experiences by God's revelation in the Bible. For more details, see the chapter in this book on discernment.

The drift of pinions, would we hearken,
Beats at our own clay-shuttered doors.

For Further Reading

Adler, Mortimer J. *The Angels and Us.* New York: Collier/Macmillan, 1982.

Anderson, Joan Wester. *Where Angels Walk.* Sea Cliff, New York: Barton and Brett, 1992.

Dickason, C. Fred. *Angels, Elect and Evil.* Chicago: Moody Press, 1975.

Freeman, Eileen Elias. *Touched by Angels.* New York: Warner Books, 1993.

Graham, Billy. *Angels, God's Secret Agents.* Waco: Word Inc., 1986.

Malz, Betty. *Angels Watching Over Me.* Old Tappan, NJ: Revell, 1986.

MacDonald, Hope. *When Angels Appear.* Grand Rapids: Zondervan, 1982.

Ronner, John. *Do You Have a Guardian Angel?* Murfreesboro, TN: Mamre Press, 1985.

Publications

Angel Watch, P.O. Box 1362, Mountainside, NJ 07092. Bimonthly sixteen-page magazine with news about angels and their work in the world today. Sixteen dollars annual subscription.

Marilynn's Angels 275 Celeste Drive, Riverside, CA 92507. The first mail-order catalog devoted exclusively to angel articles from stationery to collectibles. Annual subscription, one dollar. From Marilynn Webber, author of this book.

National Clubs

Angel Collectors Club of America. 16342 West Fifty-fourth Street, Golden, CO 80403.

Angels for All Seasons, a shop filled with angel items. Bill and Sally Allen, owners. 3100 Sheridan Place, Denver, CO 80227.

Angels of the World. 1236 South Reisner Street, Indianapolis, IN, 46221.